THE FUTURE OF THE SOVIET ECONOMIC PLANNING SYSTEM

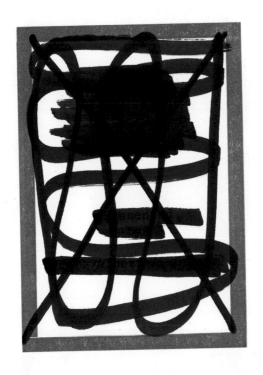

THE FUTURE OF THE SOVIET ECONOMIC PLANNING SYSTEM

DAVID A. DYKER

M.E. Sharpe Inc.
Armonk, New York

M. E. Sharpe, Inc.
80 Business Park Drive
Armonk, New York 10504 USA

Library of Congress Cataloging-in-Publication Data

Dyker, David A.
    The future of the Soviet economic planning system.

    Bibliography: p.
    1. Soviet Union—Economic policy—1917–
    2. Central planning—Soviet Union. I. Title.
HC335.D87   1985   338.947   84-27594
ISBN 0-87332-324-6
ISBN 0-87332-479-X (pbk.)

CONTENTS

Contents

FIGURES

TABLES

Figures and Tables

PREFACE

This book is the fruit of fifteen years of teaching courses on economic planning, and on the Soviet economy. Thus my first acknowledgement must be to my students, past and present, whose contribution has been as substantial as unsuspecting. More specifically, I have to thank Professor Peter Wiles of the London School of Economics and Dr Peter Holmes of the School of European Studies, University of Sussex, who read the typescript and made many useful criticisms. The book is certainly the better for their interventions. I am grateful to Cambridge University Press for allowing me to use material from my *Process of Investment in the Soviet Union*, to Academic Press, Inc., for extending me the same freedom in relation to my 'Decentralization and the command principle - some lessons from Soviet experience' article, published in *Journal of Comparative Economics*, *5*, no. 2, and to the NATO Economics and Information Directorates which gave me permission to re-present some of the material I used in 'Planned and unplanned investment patterns in the 1980s', published in *The CMEA Five-Year Plans (1981-1985) in a New Perspective* (NATO, Brussels, 1982). The Institute of Development Studies, University of Sussex, was equally obliging in connection with my 'Soviet agriculture since Khrushchev — decentralisation and dirigisme', *IDS Bulletin*, *13*, no. 4. Last but not least, my thanks are due to the secretarial staff of the School of European Studies, University of Sussex, who typed the manuscript so efficiently.

1 THE HISTORICAL ORIGINS OF THE SOVIET PLANNING SYSTEM

Introduction

In an age when we still largely identify planning, at least in its centralised form, with the Soviet Union, it is worth reflecting on the fact that the birth of the Soviet planning system predates the emergence of any substantial body of planning theory by some decades. The Marxian classics say little about socialist planning except that it would be necessary (Marx, 1968; Engels, 1962), and Lenin seems to have been half contemptuous, half unaware of the problem of *managing* a planned economy (Lenin, 1966). Lev Kantorovich published a preliminary account of his seminal work on linear programming in 1939 (Kantorovich, 1939), but did not develop it fully until after the Second World War. The parallel American work on linear programming was first developed in 1947 (Dorfman *et al.*, 1958, p. 3). Economists like Kritsman, who worked in Gosplan, the State Planning Commission, during the 1920s, made substantial progress with the ideas of iteration and linkage as a way of understanding the interrelationships of the economy (Kritsman, 1921), but though Wassily Leontief was working in the Soviet planning establishment in the early 1920s he did not publish his first discussion of the Input-Output technique until 1936 (Leontief, 1936). Again, as with linear programming, full development of this piece of theoretical apparatus had to wait until after the war. If we want to understand where Soviet planning comes from, then we have to look, not in books, but at the circumstances of the year 1930.

That was the year in which the first five-year plan really got under way. It was in December 1929 that the decision was taken to try to fulfil the plan nine months ahead of schedule, the first major operational impetus in Stalin's strategy of 'planning for the impossible'. It was around the same time that heavy industrial targets were upped, while light industrial targets were reduced, heralding the arrival of the 'priority principle' as a key tactical element in the Soviet economic system (Nove, 1969, pp. 187-9). January 1930 saw the beginning of a bloodily coercive collectivisation campaign which would leave no one in doubt as to what the 'command principle' was to mean under Stalin. It is surely not an exaggeration to say that, material incentives or no,

1

Table 1.1: Industrial Production in Selected Industrial Branches, 1913 and 1926

	1913	1926
Coal (millions of tons)	29.0	27.6
Electricity (millions of kWh)	1,945	3,508
Pig iron (thousands of tons)	4,216	2,441
Steel (thousands of tons)	4,231	3,141
Cotton fabrics (millions of metres)	2,582	2,286

Source: Nove, 1969, p. 94.

under-fulfilment of plans in the 1930s was simply viewed as treason (Nove, 1969, pp. 216–18). This obsession with growth and structural change at all costs was, of course, a reflection not only of Stalin's politics, but also of the economic conditions of the time.

The Soviet Union in the 1920s was an industrialising country, but it was industrialising slowly, and from a low base. The First World War, the Revolution and the Civil War took a terrible toll of production potential, and aggregate industrial production in 1926 was not much higher than it had been in 1913. Table 1.1 presents figures for physical production in some key sectors.

Thus Soviet coal output in 1926 was a little below that of Bulgaria in 1982: Soviet steel output in 1926 was slightly above that of its little Black Sea ally in 1982 (Economic Commission for Europe, 1983, p. 163). In 1926 26.3 million people out of a total population of 147 million lived in towns, with about 11 million in non-agricultural employment (Nove, 1969, pp. 145 and 267). There was widespread rural overpopulation, and while it is impossible to be precise, we must presume that the marginal product of agricultural labour was very low. The savings/investment ratio was around 12.5 per cent of national income in 1928 (Gregory and Stuart, 1981, p. 386). Repudiation of the international debts of the Tsarist regime, coupled with the difficult international economic conditions of the post-Wall Street crash period, ensured that any increase in the rate of accumulation would have to be internally financed. Natural conditions were not conducive to high levels of agricultural productivity, with long cold winters, drought problems in the south, and acid soils in the north. Endowment with industrial raw materials was, by contrast, extremely good. Coal was abundant in the Donbass (Ukraine) and Kuzbass (Western Siberia), oil in Transcaucasia and the Volga region: the Urals were rich in ferrous and non-ferrous metals. In some ways, then, the Soviet Union *c*. 1930 was a typical developing country, with a relatively low level of accumulation and substantial surplus agricultural population. But she could not count on large-scale capital transfer from abroad – for better or worse. More unequivocally, she had a firm, if small, industrial base, and the kind of raw material endowment which ensures that industrialisation drives did not lead straight to balance of payments problems.

It stood to reason, then, that Soviet planning had to be planning for development – in the first instance planning to *create* industry rather than planning how to *run* industry: and just as Soviet planning in practice predates most modern theory of planning, so the Soviet approach to development predates most modern development theory. But here there was a Marxian literature, originating largely in the debates of the 1920s in the Soviet Union itself. The principal protagonists in those debates, Nikolai Bukharin and Evgenii Preobrazhenskii, took up positions which could be more or less identified with, respectively, the 'balanced growth' and 'unbalanced growth' schools in post-war development economics. This is not the place to go into detail on a fascinating episode of intellectual history (see Erlich, 1960; Jasny, 1972). But Stalin's strategy for growth was essentially a rather crude version of the Trotskyist Preobrazhenskii's theory. Development was identified with industrialisation, industrialisation would be impossible without capital-intensive techniques, which meant high savings/investment ratios. In the absence of any chance of foreign loans this meant that some kind of 'primitive socialist accumulation' (Preobrazhenskii's phrase) or 'pumping-over' (Stalin's phrase) at the expense of the numerous, if impoverished, peasantry would be a necessary condition of any sharp increase in the rate of accumulation. Development would be essentially autarkic in relation to *production*, if not in relation to *technology*. That presented no problems as far as raw material supplies were concerned, but it did mean that processing capacity would have to be a priority. It also meant that the Soviet Union would have to build up its engineering industry at top speed, simply to provide the machines to raise the investment ratio. It is not difficult in this context to understand why Stalin laid such stress on heavy industry. High rates of growth of national income were viewed partly as an end in themselves, partly – certainly by Preobrazhenskii – as a means of ensuring a rapid increase in employment (there were 1.6 million registered unemployed in 1929 (Nove, 1969, p. 115)).

We have to be a little careful about identifying the idea of Stalinist development strategy with the outcome. Collectivisation was implemented with such clumsy brutality that a great deal of capital stock, including livestock, was destroyed. Though net investment in agriculture was low throughout the Stalin period, substantial capital inputs had to be made throughout the 1930s to compensate for the losses incurred during collectivisation − tractors to replace horses, for example. Recent research suggests that there was, in fact, a net 'pumping-over' *into* agriculture in the 1930s (Ellman, 1979, pp. 92−6). And if creation of employment was a goal, then results over the first five-year plans were almost embarrassingly successful. Total non-agricultural employment was planned to reach 15,764,000 by 1932−3, but in fact reached 22,804,000, with employment in large-scale industry and construction rising to almost twice the planned level (Nove, 1969, p. 195).

Development economists have in fact pin-pointed duality in technology, with main-line activities being developed on a highly capital-intensive basis and auxiliary operations continuing on a highly labour-intensive basis, as a key feature of Soviet development patterns (Wilber, 1969, Ch. 5). Now there is nothing in the Preobrazhenskii-Stalin line of thought to give this *ex ante* legitimacy − rather it was Bukharin who had talked about the value of intermediate technology. In any case, as we shall see later, the peculiar form that dual technology takes in the Soviet Union is a largely unintended effect of certain characteristic weaknesses in the planning system. Nevertheless on balance early Soviet industrialisation was a fairly labour-intensive process, with labour productivity growing at much more modest rates than national income. Table 1.2 summarises output and input trends, as recalculated in Net National Product (NNP) terms by Abram Bergson.

We immediately encounter the classic index number problem: outputs can only be aggregated on the basis of a chosen set of prices, and different price weights may produce quite different aggregate output estimates. We should not be surprised that rates of growth of national income calculated predominantly in early-year prices are much higher than rates calculated in late-year prices, since prices of the new products which give the impetus to economic growth tend to be high on first introduction, then fall sharply as mass production is developed. The contrast between the two NNP figures in Table 1.2 does, indeed, serve to highlight the dramatic extent of structural change in the Soviet economy over this crucial decade or so. But whereas national income grew impressively at 4−9 per cent, labour productivity grew rather ordinarily at 1−5 per cent.

Even more striking is the sharply negative rate of growth of capital productivity over the given period. We would expect a substantial element of short-term diminishing returns when the volume of investment

Table 1.2: Soviet National Product, Factor Inputs and Productivity, Average Annual Rates of Growth, 1928-40

Net national product	1937 ruble factor cost	4.2
	Composite price base[a]	9.3
Employment		3.7
Reproducible fixed capital	1937 rubles	9.8
	Composite price base	11.0
Selected inputs (labour, capital, agricultural land)	1937 weights	3.8-4.2
NNP per worker	Output at 1937 ruble factor cost	0.5
	Output on composite price base	5.4
NNP per unit of fixed capital	Output at 1937 ruble factor cost, capital in 1937 rubles	−5.1
	Output and capital on composite price base	−1.6
NNP per unit of selected inputs	Outputs at 1937 ruble factor cost, inputs using 1937 weights	0.1-0.5
	Output on composite price base, inputs using 1937 weights	4.9-5.3

Note: a. With rates of growth 1928-37 calculated in 1928 prices, and rates of growth 1937-40 calculated in 1940 prices.
Source: Bergson, 1978, p. 122.

rises as rapidly as 14.5 per cent per annum (Gregory and Stuart, 1981, p. 337). But in the context of almost unlimited long-term investment opportunities capital was never anything else but a very scarce resource in the Soviet Union of the 1930s. With the wholesale introduction of new technologies from the West, furthermore, the production possibility frontier was being moved outwards all the time. Thus the capital productivity figures for the period 1928-40 are surprisingly unimpressive. To make sense of this we have to move from the strategic to the tactical level, from the conceptual to the implementational.

Centralisation and the Command Principle

It is not difficult to see why Stalin favoured a quasi-military, command approach in strategic decision-taking. He was obsessed with speed, and even Winston Churchill discovered that when you want something very different done very quickly you have to give people orders (see Devons, 1950). At the level of specific tasks for specific sectors and enterprises, too, there is a strong theoretical case for using direct instructions as a basis for plan implementation. The pioneers of the post-war period developed theorems permitting the derivation of optimal sets of prices from optimal sets of outputs: thus a planning board would be able to operate a system of indirect centralisation, calculating optimal prices and simply telling its enterprise managers to maximise profits. Now of course the Soviet planners of the 1930s did not have these theorems at their disposal, neither did they have the computers without which major planning operations of this kind are not possible.

But the theorems do in any case suffer from very serious limitations – in particular they cannot cope with externalities and increasing returns. If a given level of aggregate output is to be specified there is no alternative to specifying corresponding disaggregated levels of output. Contemporary theorists have come up with sophisticated proposals for combining price and output planning (Heal, 1973), but it is obvious why the Soviet planners of the 1930s took a simpler approach. Faced with politically determined aggregate targets – for key sectoral production series rather than national income – they proceeded on the basis of essentially arithmetical division and sub-division of tasks among administrative intermediaries and enterprises. This kept their own life as simple as possible, and it provided easily understood targets for unsophisticated managers and workers – not just easily understood, but easily assimilable, since they related the particular to the general in a very obvious way.

Even so, the sheer volume of planning operations imposed on the central planners was such as to make it impossible to do all the strictly necessary calculations properly. Although the hierarchy of Soviet planning developed into a fairly neat, three-tiered system, running Gosplan-sectoral ministry-enterprise, it is important to note that this was in no way a multi-level planning system in the sense used by Kornai (Kornai, 1969). Rather than just disaggregating down to the intermediate level and leaving the ministries to do the rest, Gosplan was responsible for production planning right down to the level of individual commodities. The State Planning Commission had no executive power, however, and this is where the ministries came in. It was their job to give Gosplan's targets an organisational dimension, by translating them into specific targets for specific enterprises, and to ensure that those enterprises pulled their weight. But the ministries

Figure 1.1: The Organisational Structure of the Soviet Economy, *c.* 1930–57

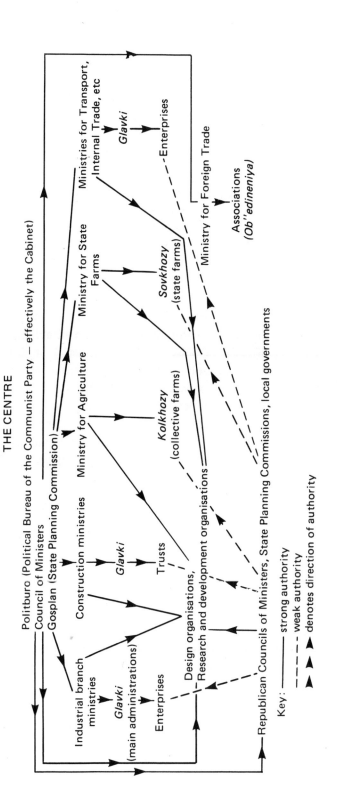

THE CENTRE

Politburo (Political Bureau of the Communist Party — effectively the Cabinet)

Council of Ministers

Gosplan (State Planning Commission)

Industrial branch ministries

Construction ministries

Ministry for Agriculture

Ministry for State Farms

Ministries for Transport, Internal Trade, etc

Ministry for Foreign Trade

Glavki (main administrations)

Glavki

Glavki

Enterprises

Trusts

Kolkhozy (collective farms)

Sovkhozy (state farms)

Enterprises

Associations (*Ob"edineniya*)

Design organisations, Research and development organisations

Republican Councils of Ministers, State Planning Commissions, local governments

Key: ——— strong authority
- - - - weak authority
▲ ▲▲ denotes direction of authority

were entrusted with the actual planning of only a few hundred commodity groups, of mainly intra-sectoral significance.

This did not stop the ministries from developing into very powerful institutions — as we shall see in Chapter 5 their role in the investment field has always been crucial. Rather it is merely to say that the nature of the division of labour between Gosplan and the ministries meant a great deal of overlap between the two instances in terms of the planning and assignment of commodity targets, and that meant that the central planners had to try to cope with some thousands of product groups. Given the limited computational technology of the time it was therefore quite impossible for Gosplan staff to work out the full implications of any adjustments to plans that might have to be made. Their Material Balances method of plan construction illustrated in Table 1.3 has the simplicity and convenience of double-entry bookkeeping, and its attractions to computerless planners are obvious. But because it does not lay out the information in matrix form, it provides no direct basis for calculating secondary effects of changes in particular plan magnitudes.

The planning process as it evolved in the 1930s would start with a set of very rough 'control figures' (*kontrol'nye tsifry*) which the centre would send down through the hierarchy of ministry and enterprise, and on the basis of which producing units would make their preliminary requests for supplies. What happens when projected supply and demand for product X do not quite match? In principle adjustments should be made not only to planned levels of output of the inputs into product X, but also to planned levels of inputs into those inputs, and so on for a certain number of iterations which will be determined by the structure and complexity of the economy. But whereas all this can be done on the basis of a single Input-Output table, it may involve looking at dozens of Material Balances, the interrelations between which are not clearly shown. Understandably, then:

> Because the calculation of changes in the Material Balances is very labour-intensive, and because in practice there is not enough time for the completion of such work, sometimes only those balances which are linked by first-order relationships are adjusted. As regards relationships of the second order, never mind those of the third and fourth order, adjustments in the balances are made only in cases where the magnitudes involved are large. (Efimov, 1957, p. 107)

Certainly the characteristically Stalinist habit of starting the planning process from key intermediate goods rather than final goods reduces the number of iterations required for a given level of consistency.

Table 1.3: Material Balance for Product X (in hundreds of thousands of tons)

Resources	Distribution
(1) Production (subdivided by republics)	(1) Production needs (subdivided by republics and by ministries)
(2) Imports	(2) Free market allocation[a]
(3) Other sources	(3) Exports
(4) Stocks at suppliers at beginning of plan period (subdivided by republic)	(4) Other needs
	(5) Stocks at suppliers at end of year
	(6) Reserves

Note: a. Free market allocation refers to supplies which go outside the sphere of state-sector production, i.e. all goods for final consumption, and also producer goods for the collective farm sector.
Source: Ellman, 1970, p. 87.

Nevertheless in practice Soviet plans are often not even approximately consistent; in the purely technical sense Soviet planning has always been *over-centralised*. Now the Marxian classics are certainly predominantly centralist in tendency: yet we must surely seek essentially functional explanations for the extraordinary persistence of this feature of Soviet planning. These seem to fall into two categories.

Firstly, over-centralisation may have a rationale in terms of the resource endowment situation of the early period of planning; it certainly does have one in terms of the operation of the command principle. Shortage of trained managers is a characteristic of the resource endowment situation in all developing economies, and Stalin had made things worse with his purges of 'bourgeois specialists'. A high degree of centralisation may have permitted the authorities to concentrate what cadres they had to maximum effect. Certainly it allowed them to use men with no managerial training as factory directors. On the other hand, it tied up middle-level administrators in bureaucratic wrangling, leaving them less time to be effective captains of industry. Less equivocally, one cannot in practice operate the command principle throughout an industrial economy unless one is prepared to work at a very high level of centralisation. Specificity is the essence of target planning, for once we get beyond the agrarian, semi-subsistence level the scope for distortion of ill-defined output targets is almost unlimited, as we shall see later on. But if sufficiently clear instructions are to be issued for every major product group and for every producing unit, and in the absence of multi-level planning, then the centre cannot but be saddled with a colossal burden of work. With multi-level planning much of this burden could be devolved to intermediate planning bodies, but relationships between centre and intermediate level would then have to be organised at least partly on a parametric basis (see Chapter 3 below). So if pure command principle is wanted – and as we have seen there were substantial reasons for wanting just that – a degree of over-centralisation will have to be tolerated.

But, secondly, the system was in practice in any case a good deal more flexible than our initial sketch suggests. Whatever the algebraic limitations of the Material Balances method, it has the great virtue that it does not fetishise reported Input-Output coefficients. In an economy going through as rapid a process of structural transformation as the Soviet one during the 1930s it would be quite unreasonable to assume fixed I-O coefficients. With a number of industries, e.g. the vehicle industry, being built up virtually from scratch, and with major new capacities being commissioned everywhere, economies of scale were naturally of substantial importance. Equally important, the novice industrial work-force introduced a volatile dimension into productivity trends which must have made them often impossible to plot: 'much damage was done by sheer clumsiness: expensive imported machines were smashed by inexperienced labourers or unqualified substitute-engineers' (Nove, 1969, p. 197).

Given all this it is easier to understand why planners were so blasé about leaving 'holes' in the plan. It is also easier to understand why they were prepared to turn consistency problems into a vehicle of *taut planning*. Where gaps in plans appeared, ministries and enterprises would normally be told simply to produce more with given planned inputs, or the same with fewer inputs. Downwards adjustment was avoided if at all possible. Thus pressure for maximum output was applied in a situation where the concept of full capacity had little meaning. Ministries would be left to juggle with their array of production capacities, and enterprise targets were (indeed still are) frequently chopped and changed throughout the year.

If bottlenecks proved unamenable to this treatment, the ultimate fail-safe was the priority principle. We saw on p. 1 how, right from the start, Stalin was prepared to play around with production targets in the interests of the heavy-industrial core of the economy. Throughout the 1930s and 1940s the priority principle was used consistently as a basis for ensuring that *input* flows would ultimately correspond to those output requirements. Thus, if plan fulfilment in priority sectors was threatened, resources would simply be physically shifted across to them from the 'soft' sectors – usually agriculture and light industry. Plans for the latter were often substantially underfulfilled during the

1930s (Hunter, 1964). In other words, the planners were quite prepared, *in extremis*, effectively to decentralise much of the system, as non-priority sectors were implicitly left to fend for themselves. In agriculture Stalin even countenanced the creation of a small, subsidiary private sector — to a great extent in order to ensure that peasants did not starve to death under the rigours of the priority principle. Thus there can be no priority principle without the principle of command. And the obvious wastefulness of the priority principle, as resources are directed and redirected without regard for the logic of continuous production processes, is itself a reflection of the nature of taut planning — as a tactic, not of resource *allocation*, but of resource *mobilisation*.

The Theory and Practice of Resource Mobilisation

As we move from the general to the particular in our analysis of classical Soviet growth tactics, we have to pose three major questions: first, how exactly do we expect taut planning to extend production possibilities? Secondly, what are the mechanics whereby the abundant resources of labour and industrial raw materials are mobilised? Thirdly, where does the 'scarce' factor of capital fit into all this? Post-war development theory can give us substantial help in relation to the first question.

In his *Strategy of Economic Development* (1958) Albert Hirschman proceeded from a strategic concept based on unbalanced growth to develop the notion of *linkage*. He used this to explain what an un-balanced growth path means at the level of the sector and the firm. 'Leading' projects would create *backward linkage*, by creating techno-logically determined demands for inputs — thus, for example, the setting up of a vehicle plant would create a derived demand for metals, plastics, automatic control mechanisms, etc. They might also create *forward linkage*, in the vehicles case by making possible the develop-ment of all sorts of transport services. Now Hirschman's theory was developed to interpret market economies, not command economies, and it is clear that the concept of forward linkage is of limited relevance to Soviet-type economies. For an enterprise manager concerned pri-marily with fulfilling an output target, and bound to his 'planned' suppliers of inputs, the commissioning of new and more efficient capacities to produce these inputs creates little of the pressure it may create in a profit-oriented economy, though it may certainly bring some relief. The notion of backward linkage, by contrast, seems to provide a neat theoretical underpinning for the tactic of taut planning as a way of maximising output in the short term, given spare capacity. And while in a developing market economy there is always the danger that backward linkage effects will be dissipated through imports, leading to balance of payments crises and stop-go growth patterns, the heavily autarkic Soviet approach ensured that they would be kept within the system. Of course in a Soviet context we are not just talking about pressure exerted by planners on producers. Taut planning operates as much as anything through the application of pressure by one set of planners on another — 'goading the goaders' in Alec Nove's memorable phrase (Nove, 1968, p. 308).

How exactly does this tactical element tie in with the overall strategy for growth as adopted in the Soviet Union? Using Input-Output tables covering the United States, Italian and Japanese economies, Chenery and Watanabe calculated coefficients of the ratio of purchased inputs to the value of total production for a given sector (u_j), and the ratio of intermediate to total demand for a given sector (w_i) (Chenery and Watanabe, 1958). If we interpret the former as a coefficient of backward linkage, and the latter as a coefficient of forward linkage, then we have a basis for assessing the linkage potential of particular sectors of the economy. By adding the two together we can obtain a coefficient of total linkage. Sure enough, we find that the industries with the highest total linkage coefficients include most of Stalin's favourites — iron and steel, non-ferrous metals, oil and oil products, coal products, gas, and metals and coal mining. As Wilber points out, machinery would have done much better in the Chenery and Watanabe tables if finished equipment had been counted as intermediate rather than final production. Likewise electricity would have shown a much higher total linkage coefficient if Chenery and Watanabe had used Soviet statistics, because the ratio of industrial utilisation to total utilisation of electricity has historically been much higher in the Soviet Union than in the West (Wilber, 1969, pp. 89-90).

Thus overall coefficients of total linkage suggest strongly that Stalin got his sectoral mix right in terms of maximising potential linkage effects. If, however, we look only at backward linkage effects, the argument is less clear. Iron and steel is almost as impressive on backward as on total linkage, and oil and coal products more or less hold their position. But machinery, metal mining, oil and gas, and coal mining all drop out of 'Division I' on backward linkage. Unless, then, we are prepared to attach more importance to forward linkage than seems *a priori* reasonable for a command economy, the identification between high linkage coefficients and Stalin's priorities is not complete. But it works for metallurgy, and for parts of the fuel/energy complex. If, of course, we look at structure more generally, in terms of the main sectors of the economy, it is clear that industry as a whole will always exhibit much higher linkage coefficients than agriculture, trade and services, etc. Thus we can perceive here a substantial, but not total, correspondence between strategic and tactical elements in the Soviet approach to economic development.

The linkage factor helps us to place in context the uneven emphasis of the gross output (*valovaya produktsiya*) target in the traditional Soviet planning system. Cost plans there always have been, but they have been by definition of secondary importance. Under the 'classical' system overfulfilling enterprises were allowed to 'bag', if they could, supplementary resources. Thus there was always a degree of *de facto* decentralisation on the supply side, even for priority sectors, and it was through this that the impetus to backward linkage was channelled. Semi-legal supply agents called 'pushers' (*tolkachi*) would wheel and deal for scarce inputs often on a barter basis, and local Communist Party cardres too would get involved in this kind of thing when priorities were threatened in their 'parish'. The fact that the planned wages fund for a given year tended to be based on the *actual* wage expenditure of the previous year made it easy for enterprises to recruit and hold on to labour 'just in case'. Thus the typical production cycle over a one-month operational plan period would start off with a quiet ten days, as everyone recovered from the previous cycle, ten days of 'getting into it', and a final ten days of 'storming' (*shturmovshchina*), as the deadline approached.

It was in those last ten days that underemployed labour would be marshalled, perhaps new workers recruited, and pushers scour the country for key supplies. Of course even if the shadow-price of labour was zero, these new workers had to be housed, and the Soviet Union devoted 18.3 per cent of its total investment effort to housing in 1950 (Dyker, 1983a, p. 191). But living space per person in the Soviet Union has historically been on the Japanese rather than West European/North American dimension (Wilber, 1969, p. 114), and the quality of housing construction has often been poor. There can be no doubt that the residential investment costs of the formation of the new proletariat were kept down to something near a minimum, with the pioneers on the great Siberian projects like the Bratsk hydro-electric station often living in tents (Dyker, 1983a, Chapter 6).

The issue with respect to material costs is rather more complex.

Certainly the system failed to penalise, or even encouraged, wasteful use of material resources. Certainly Soviet Russia's generous industrial resource endowment meant that this wastefulness did not, on the whole directly incur net foreign currency costs, though with a different development strategy they could, of course, have exported the raw materials. Even with the given development strategy pushers and pushers' operations in any case cost money, or rather resources, and a look at the way that they operate reveals a very high-cost form of commodity brokerage indeed. As late as the 1960s we find reports of crucial supplies being flown in for an enterprise by specially chartered aircraft ('S veterkom', 1968). And surely wasteful use of resources must have run the Soviet economy into increasing short-run marginal costs, even if not absolute production constraints, as extractive and primary-processing capacity was pressurised to produce over the score? It is, in fact, very difficult to give a confident answer to this question in the absence of comprehensive data on the cost characteristics of Soviet plants in the Stalin period. But research done on the Urals-Kuzbass coal-metallurgy complex, for example, paints a picture of a project with massive initial capital costs (it accounted for 47 per cent of total investment in ferrous metallurgy in 1931) and demanding transport implications, but fairly constant operating costs over a large range of output, as the project gradually attained something like full capacity (Holzman, 1957; Clark, 1956, pp. 216–21). In any case, of course, so many new plants were being opened during the first few five-year plans that costs were being continually lowered through (borrowed) technological progress.

The way that tautness got through to these, and other, basic industrial capacities was (a) that old, obsolescent capacities would not be shut down as new capacities were commissioned, and (b) that new projects might be forced into production long before full completion, with the period from on-streaming to planned full capacity operation often very long by international standards. At the same time big projects often languished without enough customers for years after commissioning. The Bratsk hydro-electric station, for example, worked at only 20–30 per cent capacity for the first year or so after completion. The opening of a transmission line to a neighbouring town then raised the figure to 50–60 per cent (Dyker, 1983a, p. 131). This serves to underline the weakness of forward linkage in a Soviet context, but it does mean that backward linkage effects emanating from manufacturing were that much less likely to be held up by stubborn bottlenecks.

In general, then, fragmentary micro-economic data suggest that taut

Table 1.4: Annual Growth Rates of Soviet Net Material Product
(Produced), 1929–38[a]

1929	16.0	1934	15.2
1930	21.0	1935	19.2
1931	16.8	1936	29.3
1932	11.3	1937	12.0
1933	6.5	1938	8.9

Note: a. According to official Soviet statistics.
Source: Clarke and Matko, 1983, p. 7.

planning in the early period of Soviet planning did not tend to run the economy into soaring short-run marginal costs in the extractive and primary-processing industries, and this picture is confirmed by the fairly evenly sustained year-by-year growth figures for the first decade presented in Table 1.4 (note that these are official Soviet statistics, which average out to a rather higher growth rate than Bergson calculates on either price base). There was certainly a hiccup at the end of the first, and the beginning of the second, five-year plan. Though ferrous metallurgy output growth was impressive from 1928 to 1932, it fell well short of the 'impossible' plan target, and there was significantly a 30 per cent shortfall in iron ore production. But oil and coal production held up well, and the other major problem areas of this period were outside the sphere of industry proper. By 1932 transport was emerging as a major bottleneck, with targets for railway line construction grossly underfulfilled (Nove, 1969, pp. 193-4), and this must have pushed up 'true' c.i.f. costs of deliveries of bulky materials. Problems like this were never to go away altogether, and by 1938 transport bottlenecks had forced the leadership to modify the whole concept of the Urals-Kuzbass Combine. This may well have been a factor in the economic slow-down of the late 1930s, though the impact of the Great Purges (see Conquest, 1968) was probably a more crucial one.

But if characteristic Soviet developmental features ensured that there would be no serious problem of increasing marginal costs in the short run, they did so at the cost of ensuring that *average* costs for each new complex would be consistently high, particularly average capital costs. This helps us to put Bergson's capital productivity figures into perspective, and enables us to pin-point a key weakness of the Stalinist growth strategy. Unskilled labour and to an extent raw materials are properly treated as abundant factors, and consistently made the subject of mobilisatory tactics. Capital should have been treated as a scarce factor, but a number of features got in the way of this.

First, there was a good deal of sheer gigantomania, conditioned partly, perhaps, by an undiscerning application of American experience, partly by Marxist preconceptions about the role of the rate of interest under socialism. We should certainly not press this latter argument too far. Soviet planners in sectors like energy and transport, faced with alternative technology decisions involving greatly differing degrees of capital-intensity, quickly developed an approach to project appraisal which still forms the basis of officially approved investment effectiveness criteria (see Chapter 5 for details). But these criteria were not permitted to affect strategic decisions on inter-sectoral allocation of investment funds or lists of 'leading' projects. It has been estimated that by 1940 c.i.f. costs of Soviet cement were 35-40 per cent greater than they would have been under an optimal locational pattern because plants had been built too big, in the absence of substantial economies of scale. As a result, unit transport expenditures on cement were 70 per cent higher than they should have been in that year (Abouchar, 1967).

Secondly, ministries and enterprises, faced with exacting, sometimes unpredictably exacting, output targets, envinced a strong tendency to overbid for investment resources. The fact that up to 1965 the great bulk of investment funds to state organisations was disbursed in the form of non-returnable budgetary grants — in a word that capital was a free good to the ministry or enterprise — obviously facilitated this. The best way to ensure an ample flow of resources in period $t + 1$ in a bureaucratic set-up is to get as many projects as possible started in period t, even to the extent of starting things that are not actually in the plan. And given the perennial supply uncertainty which is inevitable in the context of taut planning and 'success-indicators' which put all the emphasis on production rather than satisfaction of clients' needs it was in any case in the interests of ministry or enterprise to have as many projects as possible on the go, so that it would always have something it could be getting on with and finishing. This was one of the main reasons for the chronic tendency to *raspylenie sredstv* — 'excessive spread of investment resources' — too many projects going on at any one time, very high volumes of unfinished construction, i.e. 'frozen' capital, and average lead-times, from inception to full-scale production, of two or three times what is normal in the West (Dyker, 1983a, pp. 36–8).

Thirdly, the peculiarly Soviet pattern of duality in technology was inherently wasteful of capital, whatever it did for the utilisation of the labour force. Ministries and enterprises, looking for ways of safeguarding themselves against the effects of supply uncertainty, would seek to divert investment resources towards 'do-it-yourself' operations, thus increasing their degree of organisational autarky. Enterprises could do this perfectly legally on a very small scale through use of the *Director's* or *enterprise fund*. Ministries could do it legally on a fairly large scale because for so-called 'below-limit' investment they merely received block votes from the centre, leaving them a large measure of freedom in relation to choice of actual projects. The 'limit' appears to have been around 1 million rubles during the Stalin period. In any case, however, ministries have always been prepared to fiddle estimates so that projects properly falling into the 'above-limit' category should in fact go through the books as below-limit (see below, Chapter 5).

As a result, locational patterns became in many cases seriously distorted. In engineering most nuts and bolts and castings production became concentrated in enterprise 'dwarf-workshops', ill-equipped, certainly, in most cases, but utilising what equipment they had poorly. Ministries constrained to operate a nation-wide network of plants tended to use small plants in peripheral regions as 'dwarf-workshops writ large' (Dyker, 1983a, pp. 150–7). This often meant excess capacity, neglect of regional developmental considerations, and highly transport-intensive supply patterns, with small plants in Tashkent or Vladivostok sending components to a main-activity factory in Moscow or Leningrad. Some sectors virtually lost their organisational identity under pressure of the rapacity of the more powerful ministries. In 1957 only 386 out of a total of 15,000 sawmills in the Soviet Union were under the control of the Forestry Ministry (Fridenberg, 1957, p. 50).

In sum, then, capital tended to be used wastefully because of its key role as an *instrument of mobilisation*. There is absolutely no evidence whatsoever of any systematic planning of overall investment ratios (I/Y) or national and sectoral capital-output ratios (Y/I) until a very late date in Soviet economic history. Rather investment planning proceeded as an essentially autonomous activity in terms of sectoral and project priorities. This, coupled with the operational obsession with short-term, rather than medium-term, output results, bred an insensitivity to the problem of lead-times amongst planners at central and ministerial level. It was only in 1979 that annual breakdowns of construction work were for the first time included in the so-called 'title list' (*titul'nyi spisok*) – the key summary project planning document which has to be approved by the centre for above-limit projects (Ivanov, 1979). This blind spot in turn encouraged a blasé attitude to cost considerations at the level of the design organisation (*proektnaya organizatsiya*) entrusted with the elaboration of detailed documentation and drawings.

> Design workers know that in the majority of cases the completion of a new factory will take three, five, or even ten years, and that consequently control over estimated production costs is really not possible. As far as estimated capital cost is concerned, it will in any case be reconsidered in the course of construction. (Ferberg, 1966, p. 41)

Stalin got away with wasteful use of capital (a) because resources were so abundant, and because the mobilisatory campaign was largely successful; (b) because he was prepared to push up rates of accumulation and push down levels of consumption beyond what is normally considered acceptable. Between 1928 and 1935 the ratio of gross fixed investment to GNP grew from 12.5 to 32 per cent (Gregory and Stuart, 1981, p. 386). In 1932, a couple of years after the start of the collectivisation drive, the Soviet countryside was in the grip of a famine that cost the lives of millions of peasants.

> The immediate cause of [the famine] was not poor harvests but the requisitioning of grain from moderate harvests in such quantities that not enough was left for the peasants themselves. The main reasons for this drastic policy appear to have been, first, the attempt to maintain exports of agricultural produce and hence imports of machinery . . . (Hanson, 1968, p. 36)

The Command Principle and the Work-force

We associate the name of Stalin with terror and forced labour, and there can be no doubt that there was a significant degree of direct militarisation of labour in the early Stalin period. By the late 1930s there were several million people in Soviet labour camps. Legislation was introduced in the late 1930s and early 1940s which made provision for the direction of 'free' labour, especially of apprentice labour, and placed serious obstacles in the way of any worker wishing to change his job. Peasants on collective farms were subjected to 'organised recruitment' (Orgnabor) for industrial work, but in practice Orgnabor had little difficulty in fulfilling its quotas, as young country people in particular jumped at the opportunity to get away from the hated collective farms. The negative control imposed by passport restrictions, whereby a peasant could not leave his farm without express permission, was in practice the more onerous. The restrictive measures affecting urban labour fell into disuse after the war, being finally repealed in 1956, and though automatic issuance of passports to peasants only came in the late 1970s, organised recruitment on the old pattern did not survive the war.

Thus even under high Stalinism the bulk of the working population was constrained by essentially negative controls, with the problem of excessive labour turnover (*tekuchest'*) very much in mind, rather than active direction as such. To this day the police *propiska* (residence permit) regulations are used to stop too many people drifting into the big towns, especially Moscow, in speculative search for work. Sometimes the command principle would boil over from the production sphere into the labour sphere. As late as 1968 there was a report of all the boys at a particular school being 'directed' into the building trade by the local political establishment ('A esli . . .', 1968). This was improper, and was reported with extreme censure. We must presume, however, that hierarchies themselves under pressure from superiors to report plan fulfilment may well have indulged in this kind of thing with some regularity under Stalin. In addition, of course, Communist Party members and new university graduates were, and still are, quite legally the subject of positive direction.

But if labour was not largely directed, how was it allocated? Not surprisingly, through the market dimensions of wages and bonuses. There is nothing in classical Marxian theory to say that distribution should not be according to work rather than need throughout the intermediate period of socialism leading up to the establishment of full communism (Marx, 1968), and Stalin did not, of course, claim that even socialism had been built until 1936. Between 1928 and 1934 the decile ratio (i.e. the ratio of the total earnings of the top 10% of earners to the total earnings of the bottom 10% of earners) for all workers other than collective farmers grew from 3.8 to 4.2. By 1946 it had risen to 6.0 (Wiles, 1981, p. 25). The variable element was very substantial for management workers, with their bonuses in the top priority iron and steel industry coming to 51.4 per cent of their basic salary in 1947 (Berliner, 1966, p. 116), but it was substantial also for line workers, through the medium of bonuses and various forms of payment-by-results (PBR) schemes. We should not exaggerate the importance of financial inducements in a situation where supplies of many basic consumer goods and services were in gross deficit at fixed prices. On the other hand, privilege − for example access to various kinds of special shops − has always tended to go along with, and reinforce, differentials in wage packets in the Soviet Union (Matthews, 1978).

But however effective material incentives may have been in relation to *effort* (of this more in the next chapter), we must raise a substantial question-mark over their effectiveness in terms of *allocation* of labour. When unemployment was officially 'abolished' in the Soviet Union, around 1932 or 1933, so were labour exchanges. For the next 35 years or so job information would be purveyed largely through the medium of radio announcements, posters, etc., and recruitment done largely at the factory gate. In the post-war period Orgnabor turned increasingly towards the mobilisation of labour for work in the pioneer eastern regions, but on the whole workers thinking of changing jobs had little choice but to go 'on the road' to look for something new, and this helps to explain the problem of excessive job turnover. Planners were often as ill-informed as workers about conditions on the labour market. Soviet researchers working in the 1960s set themselves to discover why, despite the efforts of Orgnabor and the Komsomol (the Young Communist League, which frequently organises 'volunteers' for big pioneer projects), as many people came back from Siberia as went out from 1939 to 1959. Certainly Orgnabor's post-war work has left much to be desired from the point of view of efficiency (Andriyanov, 1971), but the more fundamental explanation is quite simply that the special wage coefficients established for Siberia were in real terms illusory. A 1966 calculation showed that the cost of living in Eastern Siberia was 20 per cent above that in the Central Region, while wages were only 18 per cent higher (Gladyshev, 1966, pp. 18-19). We must presume that the Soviet planners of the 1940s and 1950s were just not aware of this fact.

In general, then, the authorities appear to have lacked the detailed knowledge required to fashion a comprehensive pattern of wage planning in the pre-reform period of Soviet development. Even today they do not seem to have at their disposal the more limited information necessary to make compulsory graduate placement an effective tool of direct labour planning. In practice, this work has been devolved to a multiplicity of departments, with predictable results, and has been a good deal compromised by the influence of high-placed parents. In any case, many graduates directed to inhospitable areas simply do not turn up (Dyker, 1981a, p. 40). On the other hand, educational planning, backed up by substantial investment, has always been a major tool of Soviet development policy. The authorities have been very prepared to apply pressure on school children and students to go into the speci- alities which would best match their abilities to the needs of the national economy. This, coupled with the on-the-job training schemes characteristic of the Stalin period, has ensured that the basic com- plexion of the labour force be in conformity with planning priorities. When it comes to the allocation of individuals to particular jobs and localities, the system has operated very crudely indeed. But this must be seen against the background of a mobilisatory development strategy. Labour productivity was not a key variable in the Stalin period — indeed on-the-job training made overstaffing in any case unavoidable — and the authorities were more interested in sheer *absorption* of people into the urban labour force than in details of allocation. Edu- cational policies ensured that the broad pattern of allocation could not go very far wrong.

Conclusion

In putting together a picture of Soviet developmental strategy we may seem to have erred on the side of apology. We must certainly disclaim any intention of implying that the chosen strategy was the best one, even with the given resource endowment. Rather we have sought to demonstrate that the strategy was internally more or less consistent. Of course, the strategy was never laid down on paper in as many words, and the history of its implementation bears the scars of a pragmatism sometimes, perhaps, misled by a crude Marxism. After all the talk about primitive socialist accumulation and pumping-over, it never happened, because Stalin made such a bloody mess of collectivisation. The politics of class war, it seems, is not conducive to the effective implementation of capital transfers. Not all the excesses on the capital investment front can be put down to the mobilisatory strategy. Giganto- mania may not be a Soviet Marxist monopoly, but the labour theory of value is certainly an impediment to the correct appraisal of capital scarcity. In addition, the eccentricities of Marxian macro-economics, and the Marxian tendency to see *capitalist* accumulation as something with an independent life of its own, must provide part of the reason for planners' insensitivity to the I/Y and Y/I coefficients. Similarly with labour planning, one cannot help feeling that labour exchanges were abolished basically because they smacked of capitalism, leaving Soviet planners an inadequate basis on which to do a rather tricky job — to plan one major dimension in price terms while most of the others are planned in output terms. Finally, the planning system which grew out of the strategy soon began to exhibit a number of key weaknesses. Here we are firmly back in the realm of the strictly functional, and of the main theme of the present work. In the next chapter we move to a more operational treatment of the Soviet planning system, as a basis for placing those key weaknesses in historical and developmental perspective.

2 SOVIET PLANNING IN PRACTICE

We saw in the last chapter that the Material Balances system gives Soviet planners a framework within which to use their common sense, rather than a computational technique as such. We saw also how the tactics of taut planning coloured the interpretation of common sense. We now have to look at some of the planning rules of thumb that emerged from all this.

The 'Ratchet' Principle

There is an inherent informational problem in any command economy. Lower-level executive bodies know that any information they let go about their own production possibilities will affect the level of plan targets in the future. If a manager wants an easy plan the watchwords are audacity about supply needs, and modesty about output potential. It is for this reason that the process whereby the control figures go down the line to enterprises and back up again to Gosplan tends to turn into a process of negotiation. Enterprises 'pour in the water' and central planners 'cut off the fat'. Ministries do both, depending on which direction they are looking. But because the central planners are *known* to cut off the fat, enterprise managers in turn feel that they are *obliged* to pour in the water. All the actors are thus effectively trapped in a behaviour pattern which not even 'socialist consciousness' can break.

What, then, are the principles on which fat is cut off? The Russians call it 'planning from the achieved level' (*planirovanie ot dostignutogo urovnya*). Given that ministries' and enterprises' statements about what they can do cannot be trusted, *extrapolation of past input and output trends is used as a surrogate for direct information on production possibilities* (see Birman, 1978). Applied more specifically to growth targets, we call this the ratchet principle, as each new plan provision is calculated on the basis of a mark-up on the achieved level of the previous plan period. I believe that Martin Weitzman is wrong in specifying the ratchet principle in terms of the actual and planned performance in the previous plan period (Weitzman, 1980). I would suggest that plan targets have no *ex post* significance. Under the ratchet principle it is strictly the *achieved* level of previous periods that matters.

But why, the reader may ask, couldn't the planners evolve some kind of way of directly estimating production possibilities? Certainly in the pre-computer age it was difficult to cross-check information coming from different sources for consistency. But the primary factor here was the sheer level of centralisation of the system. It is very significant that Granick, in his econometric researches on the ministerial level in the Soviet planning system, found no evidence of the ratchet principle in centre-ministry relationships (Granick, 1980). It is manifestly easy enough for Gosplan to make direct estimates of aggregate trends in production capacity of oil, gas, electricity, etc. The problem arises when one gets down to the level of individual oil-wells and power stations. It is above all because Soviet planning is not multi-level planning, because Gosplan insists on planning by sector, but also by product, that the system is burdened with a *quantitative* informational problem to match the *qualitative* one introduced by the command principle in the first place. It is the combination of the two that makes the ratchet principle essential.

But the ratchet principle was important in other ways. The 'always up, never down' aspect is an important aspect of crude growth maximising tactics, and is obviously related to the tactic of taut planning. In addition, the ratchet helped with consistency problems. If plans, or rather outturns, were reasonably consistent last year, and if the centre applies a more or less standard mark-up all round, then this year's plans will also be reasonably consistent.

But while the ratchet principle represents an attempt to adjust to managerial behaviour patterns, it does tend itself to induce modifications in those patterns. Just as perception of the command principle induces capacity concealment, so perception of the ratchet principle induces output limitation. The best way to ensure that the target for period $t + 1$ is not too demanding is to make sure that not too much is produced in period t. And of course if a fairly easy target is obtained for period $t + 1$, it is vital that it should not be overfulfilled by too much, for fear of what might happen in period $t + 2$. Thus use of the ratchet principle encourages managers to place primary emphasis on even but modest levels of plan fulfilment.

The Micawber Principle

This is closely related to, but analytically distinct from, the ratchet principle, and brings us into the realm of specific incentive arrangements. Readers well versed in Dickens will remember Mr Micawber's salutary dictum:

> Annual income twenty pounds, annual expenditure nineteen nineteen six, result happiness . . . annual expenditure twenty pounds ought and six, result misery.

Throughout the Stalin period managerial incentive systems were strikingly asymmetrical. In principle, fulfilment would bring a substantial initial bonus, while each percentage point of overfulfilment would bring incremental bonuses. Underfulfilment by just 0.1 per cent would mean no bonuses at all, probably a reprimand, and possibly even demotion if the pattern were repeated. In practice, ministries, which administered the incentive funds, often varied the amount of money going to individual managers arbitrarily, and the only certain principle was that a non-fulfilling manager would get nothing at all (Katsenelinboigen, 1978, p. 144).

The Micawber principle is clearly basically an aspect of the crude growth maximisation approach. The underlying idea is that underfulfilment, even by a fraction, should be perceived as something essentially shameful. To that extent it merely consolidates one important aspect of the ratchet principle. If we lay great stress on the incentive to overfulfilment, of which Katsenelinboigen bids us beware, then we may look beyond the crude growth maximisation idea to perceive a more precise tie-in between Micawber on the one hand and the strategy of unbalanced growth and the tactic of taut planning on the other. If, by contrast, we see the essence of the Micawber effect in terms of placing a high premium on simply avoiding underfulfilment at any cost, then the complementarity of ratchet and Micawber is the more apparent. We should add that the application of the Micawber principle, and the perception of its application by managers, makes the ratchet more necessary, by exacerbating the tendency induced by the command principle to capacity concealment.

Ratchet and Micawber and Managerial Behaviour

Taken together, then, these two basic principles, or rather rules of thumb, of Soviet planning procedure help with informational difficulties, ease the problem of internal plan consistency, and fortify the crude growth maximisation approach. At the same time they encourage output limitation. But how can planning principles which do that possibly contribute anything to growth rates? Have we, in fact, discovered another 'wrong-headed' element in the Soviet approach to planning for development? Perhaps so, but before jumping to conclusions we will do well to look at some of the Western literature on workers' reactions to PBR schemes. Even in the United States it is normal for workers on piece rates to operate a 'bogey'. This is an unofficial quota, beyond which most workers will not produce, for fear of giving the management an excuse to 'raise the norms' (Roy, 1972). In other words, Western managements perceive that under PBR conditions workers have an incentive to conceal capacity, and try to solve the problem by observing output trends very closely; the workers realise that and tailor their output trends accordingly. This is precisely a microcosm of the situation we are analysing in relation to Soviet planners *vis-à-vis* subordinate managers. But the really interesting thing is that although this phenomenon is universal throughout the Western industrial world, a British National Board for Prices and Incomes report could conclude that 'there was wide agreement in the general evidence we received that the most usual reason for installing PBR had been to raise output, and that it had been effective in doing so' (National Board for Prices and Incomes, 1968, p. 20). Payment by results sets up conflicting pressures in a management system, but both Soviet and Western experience indicate that on balance it is good for *short-term* output trends. This, however, is by no means the end of the story.

Ratchet, Micawber and the Long Term

We introduced the phenomenon of 'storming', of uneven work tempi in Chapter 1, essentially in the context of supply uncertainty and the ways in which enterprise managements react to supply uncertainty. We should note now that under the operation of the ratchet and Micawber principles managers will have an incentive to *shturmovshchina* irrespective of any supply uncertainty. There may be perfectly normal technical reasons why monthly output indices should not be completely even, why they may be for overworked and harassed Gosplan and ministerial officials unpredictably uneven. It will always be in the interests of a manager in a Soviet-type system to try to iron out any such variations, at least as far as plan fulfilment *reporting* is concerned. This means that he may indulge in a degree of what is called in British factories 'cross-booking', where output produced (or rather hopefully produced) in period $t + 1$ is reported as being produced in period t (see Lupton, 1972). But the scope for this is limited, while the insensitivity of the traditional Soviet planning system to cost indicators meant the scope for storming was always substantial. Thus the concern to maintain even levels of plan fulfilment from one month to the next tended to exacerbate the tendency to sharply uneven tempi of production from one week to the next. A survey conducted over the period October 1965–March 1966 found that 21–29 per cent of TV sets were produced in the first ten days of the month, 30–33 per cent in the second ten days, and 39–48 per cent in the last ten days (Skorodunov, 1966, p. 14). But annual plans are also very important from the point of view of bonuses and promotion, and the storming syndrome has been correspondingly very evident in the quarterly pattern of plan fulfilment as well, particularly in sectors with longer production cycles. In residential construction, for example, over the twenty-year period 1953–73, 8–11 per cent of completions came in the first quarter, 19–21 per cent in the second quarter, 20–22 per cent in the third quarter, and 46–49 per cent in the fourth (Tsygankov, 1976).

Thus we can perceive how very deep-seated are the employment patterns characterised by overmanning and low productivity which the pressure for *shturmovshschina* engenders in the Soviet planning system. Supply uncertainty is partly a result of growth orientation and so is ratchet, while Micawber is largely related to the crude growth maximisation approach. More fundamentally, supply uncertainty and ratchet are related to over-centralisation, and therefore so is storming and all that it entails. This is a theme to which we will return repeatedly.

The other major side-effect of the operation of the ratchet and Micawber principles brings us to another crucial dimension of the Soviet, as of any other industrial, economy — research and development and innovation. Recent literature has illuminated systematic difficulties in the relationships between Soviet 'scientific-research' organisations and the shop floor (Hutchings, 1976; Amann *et al.*, 1977). It is not difficult to trace these difficulties back partly to the problem of tailoring a quantity-oriented planning system to institutions the output of which cannot possibly be measured quantitatively. What we are more concerned with here is the general problem of assimilation of new technology at enterprise level, whether that new technology originates from a Soviet R and D establishment or technology transfer from the outside world.

Clearly a command planning system must have some advantages over market systems in relation to the introduction of technical change. As we noted in the last chapter, the technological levels of most sectors of Soviet heavy industry were revolutionised with the building of a series of key new plants in the 1930s. But they were *new* plants. Where the Soviet system does less well is with the introduction of new techniques into established plants, and here we are once again back with the ratchet and Micawber effects. Of course, a planning system oriented towards crude quantity is going to take a dim view of cost-saving innovations. In 1965 a textile factory which had successfully developed some synthetic fibres failed to fulfil its gross output plan, expressed in value terms, because prices for synthetics were set at a lower level than those of conventional materials, presumably because they were cheaper to produce (Demchenko, 1965). More generally, however, *any* innovation, even if it is good for gross output, is likely to be bad news in terms of the optimal path (for the manager) of even, modest levels of plan fulfilment. Any stoppage for retooling threatens plan fulfilment in the given plan period, and a manager who is in a position to make up lost ground in the following period and earn overfulfilment bonuses will likely end up with an awful target in the period after that.

We are suggesting, then, that the undoubted technological dynamism (in implementational terms) of the early Stalin period was largely a function of the unusually high proportion of wholly new enterprises amongst the total number of investment projects. Once the Soviet economy had settled down to a more normal relationship between the two kinds of investment, the power of the command principle could no longer match the power of shop-floor defensive reaction. For this the ratchet and Micawber principles are wholly to blame. Once again, we pin-point those two principles as key obstacles to the development of high-productivity manufacturing patterns in the Soviet economy.

These technological considerations bring us into what is perhaps the major area of interest from the point of view of the operational evolution of the Soviet planning system: to what extent have the strengths of the Soviet planning system turned to weaknesses, to what extent have the weaknesses passed from venal to cardinal in the course of economic development, and as a function of the rapid growth patterns which the system was precisely designed to foster? The answers to these questions represent a crucial aspect of the background to the emergence of the economic reform movement.

The Classical Stalinist Planning System in Historical Perspective

Let us start with the most difficult of this set of issues, that of *tautness*. There is a theoretical argument to the effect that 'the longer the chain of supply relationship, the more weighty is this element [namely that tautness may increase effort, but it also introduces uncertainty, which reduces effort − D.A.D.] in favouring lower but surer targets' (Keren, 1972). This seems to fit with the suggestions of common-sense empiricism, and it represents an *a priori* argument that as an economy grows and becomes more complex, so the virtues of balance may increasingly outweigh the enticements of imbalance. In the Soviet case, however, perhaps the key variable here is the extent to which tautness has been backed up by the priority principle.

As we saw in Chapter 1, the tactical application of that principle in favour of a limited number of heavy-industrial sectors was a key feature of the Stalin period. As soon as Stalin died a process of progressive weakening of the priority principle began. To a degree this represented an 'objective' necessity, which Stalin, had he survived, would have had to face up to. The policy of unbalanced growth at the strategic, sectoral level had by the early 1950s resulted in a situation of gross disequilibrium between industry and agriculture, and Table 2.1 illustrates the long term production trends which had brought this situation about. Powell's recalculations in terms of Final Industrial Product, which nets out the substantial amount of double-counting in the Soviet Gross Industrial Output series, suggests a slightly lower figure for industrial growth over the Stalin period (Clarke and Matko, 1983, p. 204). On the other hand, despite the mobilisation of the rural population for the industrialisation effort − the urban population grew by 30 million from 1926 to 1939 (Gregory and Stuart, 1981, p. 243) − the total farm population does not appear to have dropped much in absolute terms from 1928 to 1953, so that the record on agricultural productivity was just as poor as on output (Gregory and Stuart, 1981, p. 253; Clarke and Matko, 1983, p. 35). Western research indicates much more effective 'pumping-over' of resources from rural

Table 2.1: Annual Rates of Growth of Industrial and Agricultural Gross Output, 1928–53[a]

Industry				Agriculture			
1928	18.9	1941	−2.0	1928	2.5	1941	−38.0
1929	19.7	1942	−21.4	1929	−2.4	1942	−38.7
1930	22.2	1943	16.9	1930	−3.3	1943	−2.6
1931	20.7	1944	15.6	1931	−2.6	1944	45.9
1932	14.6	1945	−15.3	1932	−6.1	1945	11.1
1933	5.2	1946	−16.3	1933	−5.6	1946	13.3
1934	19.2	1947	20.8	1934	5.0	1947	27.9
1935	22.7	1948	26.9	1935	12.3	1948	11.5
1936	28.7	1949	19.5	1936	−8.4	1949	2.1
1937	11.2	1950	22.7	1937	22.9	1950	0.0
1938	11.7	1951	16.8	1938	−10.5	1951	−6.1
1939	16.1	1952	11.4	1939	0.8	1952	8.6
1940	11.7	1953	12.0	1940	16.5	1953	3.0

Index numbers

1913 = 100, 1928 = 132, 1940 = 852   1913 = 100, 1928 = 124, 1940 = 141
1940 = 100, 1953 = 252   1940 = 100, 1953 = 104

Note: a. According to official Soviet statistics.
Source : Clarke and Matko, 1983, pp. 10–15.

to urban sectors in the period of post-war reconstruction than there had been during the original 'Great Leap Forward' (Karcz, 1968). To this extent the continuation of the agricultural price policies of the 1930s had a kind of rationale. But with an ever-increasing urban population the stagnatory trend in production could only go on for so long. In real terms the Soviet grain harvest never regained its 1940 level in Stalin's lifetime (Nove, 1969, p. 303), and Soviet leaders were talking in the early 1950s of 'the grain problem' as if they were back in 1927–8 (even if they were saying that it had been solved by 1952!).

It is not surprising, then, that the post-Stalin 'collective leadership' (Khrushchev was already in charge of agriculture, though he did not consolidate his political ascendancy until 1956–7) made immediate announcement of a series of measures designed to improve the agricultural situation. By 1954 average nominal grain prices were over 700 per cent better than they had been in 1952, and the corresponding figure for meat was nearly 600 per cent (Nove, 1969, p. 328). Better prices would not only help to finance better incomes for peasants, they would also permit the *kolkhozy*, which in principle have to finance all their own investment, to push up fixed capital formation in agriculture. That in turn meant that farm machinery and building materials output had to be increased, while land improvement schemes would require sharp increases in fertiliser output. Nor were these developments a flash in the pan. Total annual agriculture investment doubled between 1953 and 1955, and has grown remarkably steadily ever since (Clarke and Matko, 1983, pp. 17-18). The trend at the strategic level obviously weakened the priority principle as a tactical weapon, since it reduced – greatly if we bear in mind indirect effects – the number of 'soft' sectors available to take the strain when the going gets tough.

But there were other, more subjectively political, changes in the period 1953-4 which further weakened the priority principle. Town dwellers were promised not just more and better food – they were also promised a substantial increase in the supply of manufactured consumer goods. (Farmers would obviously not want to spend all *their* increased income on agricultural products.) Plans for investments in consumer manufactures were raised sharply as a back-up to this, and prices were slashed in order to create the requisite purchasing power. The primacy of the 'Law of the Faster Growth of the Production of the Means of Production' was even temporarily overturned. These specific measures were not properly thought out – prices were cut over-hastily, producing queues, while the new output targets were never met (Nove, 1969, p. 325), and were abandoned after the political demise of Malenkov in 1955. But Khrushchev never went back to the grim, belt-tightening days of Stalin, and American recalculations suggest that *per capita* consumption in the Soviet Union grew 4.5 per cent per annum in the period 1950-69, as compared to 1.1 per cent for 1928-37 (Gregory and Stuart, 1981, p. 360). And though power cuts to student hostels of several days' duration were still common when I was a student in the Soviet Union in the late 1960s, industrial supplies to private consumers would never have the same 'flexibility' again.

Did this weakening of the priority principle in an in increasingly complex economy exacerbate supply uncertainty, or force a reduction in the degree of tautness? The evidence is conflicting and inconclusive, but the answer is probably both. If we accept Khrushchev's assessment that organisational-autarkic patterns were becoming markedly worse in the mid-1950s (see Chapter 3), then we can deduce that the underlying supply problem must also have been getting worse. As we shall see later, improvement in supply conditions through changes focusing on the enterprise was a key thrust of the 1965 planning reform. This, of course, strictly proves that the problem was bad, rather than necessarily getting worse. In any case, as we argue below, there were other good reasons why the supply problem might have been getting worse. At the same time, at least part of the reason for the abandonment of the sixth five-year plan in 1957 was that it was 'over-ambitious and unworkable' (Nove, 1961, p. 67). Granick, in his study of centre-intermediate planning body relationships, found evidence of a reduction in tautness after 1965 (Granick, 1980), and a *Pravda* policy article from the late 1970s talks about 'planned reserves creat[ing] scope for economic manoeuvring within the framework of five-year and annual plans, without breaking or changing them' (Abalkin, 1977). On the other hand an Input-Output exercise carried out on the 1970 plan for Latvia revealed that it was 'impossible' (Gillula and Bond, 1977, p. 296). Planning reforms in the Soviet Union have largely been about *implementation*, while tautness/slackness is very much an aspect of plan *construction*. It has, therefore, been one of the aspects of the Soviet planning problem least aired among Soviet economists. But it keeps turning up, and we shall be returning to it.

Simpler and less controversial is the issue of *success-indicators*. The gross-output indicator has two main weaknesses. It is insensitive to costs, and it tends to encourage neglect of quality and distortion of specification, particularly in the direction of 'heaviness'. Irrigation work in the North Caucasus in the middle 1960s, for example, was vitiated by a number of characteristic faults: drainage pipes were laid only 10-15cm below the surface, instead of the normal 70cm, and the general standard of construction was so low that proper control over the system was not possible − backflows occurred, and sometimes too much water was supplied, so that land had subsequently to be drained (Kalmykov and Filipenko, 1966). It is, of course, perfectly clear that pipes are more quickly laid shallow than deep, which suits a target for metres of pipes laid. Apropos of 'heaviness', the hideousness of much Soviet architecture in the Stalin period, with its tasteless embellishments, has been blamed partly on the use of a variant of gross output as principal success-indicator in the design sector (Podshivalenko, 1965).

We have already argued at length that cost-efficiency considerations were not of paramount importance in the early days of Soviet industrialisation. We can add that the scope for quality/specification distortion in basic intermediate sectors like steel, coal, oil and electricity, producing simple, homogeneous commodities, must by definition be fairly limited. We cannot say the same thing about engineering, perhaps the most complex and heterogeneous of all main industrial production lines. Neglect of the systematic production of components and spare parts, under the pressure of the gross-output regime, has indeed been one of the major sources of supply problems in Soviet industry, and has, as we saw in Chapter 1, caused serious distortions in the locational pattern of the engineering industry itself. Nevertheless on balance it is surely fair to say that Stalin's priority sectors were not the kind likely to be too badly affected by the quality/specification weakness of the gross-output success-indicator.

The crucial changes which affected the Soviet Union in the immediate post-war period conditioned an evolution of the balance of advantages of the traditional key success-indicator, just as they presaged a transformation of the priority principle. More emphasis on consumption meant more emphasis on the little, on the quality-intensive, on the downright fussy. But just as the economy was becoming bigger and more complex, so the producer goods it required were becoming more sophisticated and more varied. In particular electronics and chemicals emerged as new key sectors for which gross output was a quite unsuitable success-indicator. Most important of all, however, the cost-insensitivity of the old indicator was becoming an increasing liability, as the Soviet economy began to run up against resource constraints. Reference forward to Table 2.4 will confirm that the Soviet labour force grew effectively by only 0.6 per cent per annum during 1956–60 according to Greenslade's recalculations. As the scope for bringing in more 'new' workers from the rural and female populations narrowed, as the rate of natural increase fell, and with the huge loss of life (at least 20 million people) during the war, it was inevitable that the labour supply situation would become tighter. The situation in that crucial first quinquennium of economic reform was exacerbated by a two-hour reduction in the working week in 1956.

As far as raw and energy materials are concerned, the crunch came rather later. Certainly problems with coal supply intensified and Caucasian oil supplies began to dry up, but Khrushchev was able to turn to the readily extractable oil resources of the Urals-Volga region, which by 1960 was accounting for 71 per cent of total Soviet oil output (Saushkin *et al.*, 1967, p. 161). By the early 1960s, however, the rate of growth of Urals-Volga oil output was slowing down, and the Soviet oil industry was being forced to move eastwards.

Commercial exploitation of gas in Western Siberia started in 1963, and of oil in 1964. Difficult natural conditions, isolated location and lack of existing infrastructure combine to push costs up sharply east of the Urals. Labour productivity on Siberian building sites is only half the Soviet average, projects take two to three times as long to complete as in the central regions of the Soviet Union, and actual construction costs of projects using standard designs exceed planned costs by 30–40 per cent. Permafrost conditions push up basic construction costs by at least 20 per cent, reduce the life-span of installations, and demand maintainance expenditures reaching 50 per cent and more of initial capital costs. Local supplies of building materials are usually inadequate, and have to be supplemented, at high cost in terms of transport, by 'imported'. On average for the oil-bearing regions of Western Siberia 6,000–7,000 rubles' worth of new investment in the non-material sphere (i.e. services, education, housing) is required for each new arrival. In the Middle Ob' area the figure is 20,000 rubles, and in the extreme north of Western Siberia around 40,000 rubles. The comparable figure for the central regions of the Soviet Union is 3,000–3,500 rubles (Dyker, 1983a, pp. 161–2).

Thus as one moves east and north in Siberia, capital costs tend to rise. But very rapid escalation of capital costs with the initiation of new hydrocarbon capacity was by no means a monopoly of Siberia, as the figures on the gas industry in Table 2.2 illustrate. Evidence has not come to hand on whether the Soviet ore-extraction industry has faced similar trends in the post-war period, although stagnating ferrous ore production was certainly one reason for difficulties in iron and steel production in the early 1980s (Dyker, 1984). In any case the evolution of the labour and hydrocarbons positions alone has radically changed the balance of mobilisatory and allocative interests, and therefore the balance of good and bad in the gross-output success-indicator.

Thirdly, we have to return to the question of *piece-work and incentives*. We noted that Western research finds payment by results the best way to get maximum short-term output, even though output limitation through the bogey is universal. Western research also tells us that when workers feel that a particular job is just not worth the trouble at the going rate, they will tend to 'goldbrick' or 'go slow', as a protest. Clearly the rates for many jobs in the Soviet Union under Stalin were very poor, and political pressure was often exerted to make them even poorer. One way to combat the bogey is through 'organised rate-busting', whereby certain individuals are 'bribed' (whether by promise of money or political favours) to break the bogeys systematically. This is essentially what the Stakhanovite movement was. (Stakhanov was a record-breaking coal-miner from the late 1930s. His records were, however, very much 'set-up jobs' (see Schwarz, 1953, pp. 193–7). Now the normal reaction to this kind of thing in Western factories would be gold-bricking. I have seen no evidence of

Table 2.2: Output-Capital Ratio (*Fondootdacha*) in the Extraction of Soviet Gas (in m³ per ruble)

	1970	1971	1972	1973
USSR	163.5	144.4	118.8	97.4
Komi ASSR	143.8	110.0	95.9	66.9
Kuibyshev and Orenburg provinces	44.8	67.2	57.5	30.0
Krasnodar province	136.8	115.0	74.8	54.5
Stavropol' province	228.3	180.6	150.1	115.3
Tyumen' province	117.5	111.1	81.7	63.2
Khar'kov province	260.6	220.1	180.7	150.3
L'vov province	126.5	118.2	99.4	146.7
Ivano-Frankovsk province	116.4	102.1	103.1	85.1
Uzbek SSR	373.2	359.9	296.3	196.6
Turkmen SSR	391.9	325.8	276.1	201.3

Source: Khashkin *et al.*, 1975, p. 40.

gold-bricking in the Soviet Union during the Stalin period, and would suggest that one of the important economic functions of Stalin's political terror may have been to discourage just that amongst the less politically motivated workers, thus ensuring that the sustained rate-busting campaign was not neutralised. To the extent that Stakhanovites were rewarded in money terms this does, by the way, help us to understand the rationale of Stalin's distribution of income.

I leave it to the political scientists to determine whether elements of political terror survived into post-Stalin Russia. If they did, they certainly do not affect ordinary workers. A 'photograph' of the working day published in *Pravda* in 1968 depicted a three-man brigade of machine operators at a Perm' factory as effectively working barely three hours in the shift (Shatunovskii, 1968). 'Socialist competitions' and 'counterpart plans' (*vstrechnye plany*) serve as a political vehicle designed to weaken the bogey (and also ease consistency problems) through raising the general level of 'involvement', but their effect has been less than decisive. A fairly recent study of disciplinary problems in the construction industry in Penza province highlighted familiar problems like heavy drinking, 'social passivity' and 'negative attitudes to work' among the proximate causes of absenteeism, loafing, etc. More interesting was the finding that disciplinary problems were more serious amongst the more senior, more highly paid workers. A picture emerges of experienced workers almost being able to work when they like (Reznik, 1980). This is in total contrast to even the mildest interpretation of the Stalin period, and it is something on which, as we shall see later, the ex-secret police chief Andropov had very strong views.

Fourthly, we must assess the impact of continuing reliance on the ratchet and Micawber principles in the context of rapid quantitative growth and qualitative evolution in the Soviet economy. From the 1960s onwards a trend sets in towards the modification of the classic Micawber principle. In that year Gosplan published a list of products for which overfulfilment was forbidden (Nove, 1961, pp. 180–1). Since 1965 overfulfilment has been more systematically de-emphasised through the introduction of reduced norms in cases of overfulfilment for deductions *into* incentive funds. Indeed regulations implemented since 1965 have introduced a fair degree of symmetry into rules for forming incentive funds, with modified coefficients being applied in cases of underfulfilment.

None of this, however, has affected the way in which actual payments *from* funds are made. Here the principle that bonuses should not be paid at all in cases of underfulfilment of key targets remains generally in force. But the tendency to de-emphasise overfulfilment does clearly get through to procedures for bonus payments, if only through the establishment of overall ceilings on total managerial bonus payments, a principle ratified *de jure* in the late Brezhnev period (Adam, 1980). Confirmation of the movement away from open-ended encouragement of overfulfilment comes in the form of a rather bizarre case, reported in 1976, in which Gosplan fined an enterprise 10 per cent of the cost of the iron used to make over-plan steel, although the iron itself was over-plan production, and all orders for iron had been met (Galkin, 1976). Of course iron and steel have in general terms been very much deficit commodities in the Soviet Union over the past decade or so. One wonders what the 'steel-eaters' of Stalin's time would have made of all this.

We should not exaggerate the importance of the transition from Micawber to 'modified Micawber' principle. As we saw earlier, the ministries under Stalin never allowed themselves to be tied down by the small print of bonus regulations when it came to rewarding their lieutenants. But the fact that post-Stalin Soviet governments have taken the trouble to issue regulations on overfulfilment suggests that the issue is of some importance in terms of indicating government preoccupations. Khrushchev was certainly just as growth-oriented as Stalin, but his initial modifications of the Micawber principle, like his abandonment of the sixth five-year plan, seem like the measures of a man who realises that the most obvious route to high growth will not be the quickest for ever — of a man faced with the totally unstalinist problem of excessive retail stocks of goods that no one wanted to buy (cf. earlier discussion of the success-indicator problem). For the first time, perhaps, the issue of 'quality of growth' came on to the Kremlin's agenda.

But, of course, the more modified is Micawber, the less there is an element of incentive for overfulfilment, the more safely we can proceed on the assumption that the two basic operational rules of Soviet planning — the ratchet and Micawber principles — induce enterprises to place the highest priority on the avoidance of underfulfilment, on the maintenance of even, modest levels of fulfilment, with all that that implies for attitudes towards work tempi, manning levels and technical change. Before going on to study how changing conditions affected the importance of these behavioural patterns, we must pause to assess how such changing conditions affected the value of Micawber and ratchet to the central planners.

As far as Micawber is concerned, we have already implicitly answered the question. The modification of Micawber clearly spelled some movement away from crude growth-maximising tactics, and corresponds to the evidence we adduced of a stuttering retreat from tautness. Had that movement been complete, Micawber could have disappeared quite painlessly. With the ratchet principle the question is more complex and interesting. To the extent that it has been an instrument of taut planning, and to the extent that planning has become less taut, ratchet must have become less important. But to the extent that it has helped with consistency problems its role must have developed over the past two or three decades, as the economy became more complex and the priority principle weakened. We can, indeed, take this argument one step further and suggest that increased reliance on the ratchet to approximate a solution to the consistency problem may have further weakened the priority principle beyond even what the post-Stalin leadership wanted, because by definition use of the ratchet for this purpose would tend to exclude the possibility of structural readjustment. We shall return to the question of rigor mortis in the structure of the Soviet economy later on. Of course crude growth maximisation tactics and consistency have never been more than subsidiary aspects of the ratchet principle. As far as ratchet's key role *vis-à-vis* the informational problem is concerned, we can discern two opposing forces at work. On the one hand, the development of computer technology and information science in general has made it easier to cross-check different bodies of information for consistency, and to build up an 'objective' picture of production possibilities. On the other hand, the growing size and complexity of the Soviet economy have obviously increased the dimensions of the information problem. All in all, then, we should not be surprised at the extraordinary resilience of the ratchet principle in the period since 1965, in the face of repeated statements from the central political authorities to the effect that it should be excised from the planners' arsenal.

We showed earlier that managerial reaction to the known use of the ratchet and Micawber principles tended to result in overmanning and resistance to technical change at the shop-floor level. We implied that the former problem must have become much more of a headache as labour shortage started to impinge. We suggested that the latter problem must have become more serious as the share of wholly new projects in total investment fell. We can add that the post-war trend towards continuous and integrated process and product innovation (see Pavitt, 1980) must have further exacerbated it. Significantly, contemporary Soviet research on technical change tends to identify innovation with the rate of introduction of new products. But is there any evidence that these problems actually became more serious *in themselves*, i.e. that storming patterns became more accentuated, that enterprise managers became less and less willing to countenance work stoppages for retooling? Here we come up against a problem of methodology. *Complaints* about these tendencies certainly became more common and more vociferous in the 1950s, but in the absence of, for example, systematic time-series on temporal work patterns in given sectors this really proves nothing. On a strictly *a priori* basis we would expect that worsening supply uncertainty would tend to make managers even more 'cagey', while any drop in the level of tautness would have the opposite effect. We simply come back, in fact, to Keren's generalised conclusions about optimal tautness. Thus it is the context rather than the essence of these problems which evolves in the post-Stalin period.

The Slow-down

It is not difficult, then, to build up a comprehensive picture of a planning system unable to keep up with the pace of evolution of its own creation, the industrialised Soviet economy. Here again we can pin-point a general weakness of the command economy: it holds no scope for any kind of Schumpeterian or Galbraithian evolution of economic institutions – for better or worse – in the face of changing economic conditions. Soviet planning and management arrangements can only be changed by *decree*, and decrees, of course, normally follow events. But our subsequent discussion of attempts at planning reform will, perforce, focus on decrees, large and small, and the manner of their implementation.

Before going on to that, we must document the deceleration in Soviet economic growth which has been implied in much of the foregoing 'qualitative' discussion. As Table 2.3 shows, the CIA is systematically sceptical about the absolute growth rates claimed by the Central Statistical Office (the definitional differences between NMP and GNP are not a substantial factor here), but the two sources do not disagree seriously on trends in growth rates. The CIA figures do tend to flatten out the pattern for the period 1951-65, and for evidence of a slowdown in the immediate post-Stalin period we really have to go to the official Soviet figures. On the other hand, both series portray a recovery of growth rates in the five years after the 1965 planning reform (though again very marginal according to the CIA), and a sharp down-turn in the 1970s. By 1983 even the official Soviet plan fulfilment report is claiming only 3 per cent.

We can more readily assess the origins of these trends if we look at the figures for factor inputs and productivity over the same period presented in Table 2.4. (Note that these are calculated in terms of a set of GNP figures which differ slightly from those in Table 2.3. In order to ensure strict comparability, we cite the five-year averages of that set of figures in the table.) Interestingly, labour productivity did not do at all badly in the 1950s, with a 5 per cent growth rate in the period 1956-60 being largely instrumental in keeping the growth rate of GNP above 5 per cent. It was the capital productivity trends for that quinquennium that really looked disturbing, with an already sharply negative rate of growth falling by a further percentage point. There can be no doubt that Khrushchev was, in general terms, aware of these trends, and this helps us to understand why he was so concerned about the capital-wasting penchants of the ministries (see Chapter 3).

In the early 1960s, however, labour productivity growth rates fell sharply, while capital productivity trends fared no better than in the previous five-year period. But it was a sharp improvement in that latter series which formed the basis of improved GNP performance in the period 1966-70, with the labour productivity growth rate

Table 2.3: The Slow-down in Soviet Economic Growth

(Average) Annual Percentage Change in NMP (Official Soviet Figures, Calculated in Constant Prices)				(Average) Annual Percentage Change in GNP (CIA Estimates, Calculated in Constant Prices)			
1951	12.2	1966	8.1	1951	3.1	1966	5.1
1952	10.9	1967	8.4	1952	5.9	1967	4.6
1953	9.8	1968	8.6	1953	5.2	1968	6.0
1954	12.1	1969	4.7	1954	4.7	1969	2.9
1955	12.0	1970	8.9	1955	8.6	1970	7.7
1951-5	11.4	1966-70	7.7	1951-5	5.5	1966-70	5.2
1956	11.4	1971	6.0	1956	8.4	1971	3.9
1957	6.7	1972	3.8	1957	3.8	1972	1.9
1958	12.6	1973	9.1	1958	7.6	1973	7.3
1959	7.4	1974	5.0	1959	5.8	1974	3.9
1960	7.7	1975	4.8	1960	4.0	1975	1.7
1956-60	9.2	1971-5	5.7	1956-60	5.9	1971-5	3.7
1961	6.9	1976	5.3	1961	5.6	1976	4.8
1962	5.6	1977	5.0	1962	3.8	1977	3.2
1963	4.1	1978	4.8	1963	-1.1	1978	3.4
1964	9.4	1979	2.6	1964	11.0	1979	0.8
1965	6.8	1980	3.2	1965	6.3	1980	1.4
1961-5	6.6	1976-80	4.2	1961-5	5.0	1976-80	2.7
		1981	3.3[a]				
		1982	2.6[a]				
		1983	3.1[a]				

Note: a. In current prices.
Sources: Clarke and Matko, 1983, p. 7; Economic Commission for Europe, 1983, p. 104; Joint Economic Committee, US Congress, 1982, pp. 55-8; *Plan Fulfilment Report for 1983*, 1984, p. 7.

remaining at its pre-1965 level. In the early 1970s both series show sharp falls, and the rate of growth of *total* productivity goes negative for the first time. That startling conclusion is rather dependent on the particular way the calculations were done, but total productivity trends would look pretty unfavourable by the early 1970s on any methodology. Thus capital productivity is the 'early turner', with Kosygin's 1965 planning reform apparently reversing the trend temporarily. It is a pity that the breakdown in Table 2.4 does not distinguish primary resources as a factor of production, but if it did we would probably find that a good deal of the sharp deterioration in total factor productivity trends during 1971-5 was ultimately imputable

Table 2.4: Average Annual Percentage Rates of Growth of GNP,
Factor Inputs and Factor Productivity, 1951–75

	1951–5	1956–60	1961–5	1966–70	1971–5
GNP	6.0	5.8	5.0	5.5	3.8
Inputs					
Total[a]	4.5	3.9	4.1	3.9	4.1
Labour (man hours)	1.9	0.6	1.6	2.0	1.9
Capital	9.0	9.8	8.7	7.5	7.9
Land	4.0	1.3	0.6	−0.3	0.9
Factor productivity					
Total	1.4	1.8	0.9	1.5	−0.2
Labour (man hours)	4.6	5.1	3.4	3.4	1.8
Capital	−2.7	−3.6	−3.3	−1.9	−3.8
Land	1.9	4.4	4.4	5.8	2.9

Note: a. Inputs have been combined using a Cobb-Douglas (linear homogeneous)
production function with weights of 60.2, 36.7 and 3.1 per cent for labour,
capital and land respectively.
Source: Greenslade, 1976, p. 279.

to diminishing returns in that area. If we want to pin-point proximate
causes of the continued decline in growth rates in the late 1970s and
early 1980s we may have to look no further than the figures for the
rate of growth of employment, which averaged 1.4 per cent during
1976–80 and 0.95 per cent during 1981–3 (Economic Commission
for Europe, 1984, Table 3.1.2). It has been estimated that diminishing
returns in primary extraction have retarded Soviet GNP growth rates by
0.6 per cent per annum during 1976–82 (Hanson, 1984).

Of course great care has to be taken in attaching ultimate 'blame'
for these adverse trends in growth rates and efficiency. We would
expect growth rates to fall off with the attainment of economic
maturity, if only because the base on which they are calculated is
getting bigger and bigger (see Gerschenkron, 1966, for a fuller discussion). We would expect some tendency for capital productivity
to fall off as the capital-labour ratio rises; the figures in Table 2.4
show that in the post-war period the Soviet capital stock has been
growing at nearly 10 per cent per annum, while the labour force has
been growing at just 1–2 per cent per annum. And can the upward
trend in Siberian energy costs really be blamed on anything else but
Mother Nature?

In fact we can reformulate all of these points to bring in the dimension of the planning system. Why has the Soviet economy faltered on
quantity without picking up substantially on quality? Given that

capital-labour ratios were bound to go on rising as labour ran short, why has technical progress not done more to keep down the capital-output ratio? And why amidst all this capital-deepening, and in the aftermath of an industrialisation drive which shows up weakest of all on productivity, has the rate of growth of labour productivity managed to *decline* by around three percentage points over 25 years? The issue of just how inexorable energy cost trends are is something we will have to come back to in Chapter 5. But there must be a presumption that a system which reports zero or negative growth in total product-ivity is in some sense badly managed. Planning reform in the Khrushchev period may well have had a depressing effect on growth rates because of its piecemeal, disorganised and disorganising character. As we shall see in the next chapter, the argument that Kosygin's 1965 reform provided a short-term fillip to growth rates can be substantiated fairly directly. But since the early 1970s the history of planning reform has been the history of what it has failed to achieve, of the trends which it has failed to reverse. We can only agree with the secretariat of the Economic Commission for Europe when it states that:

> Among the most frequently quoted qualitative factors contributing to an increase of labour productivity are the introduction of new technology, increased use of production capacities, changes in the structure of manpower skills, decrease in the number of lost working hours and days, reduced unit inputs of energy and raw material costs in general, rationalisation in management and allocation of resources, and improvement in the organisation of production processes. There are plenty of references in policy statements, plan and plan-fulfilment documents, and in the professional liter-ature . . . to this dimension of labour productivity growth, and also to the notable results obtained in this regard in many enterprises or branches. Nevertheless, the contribution of these factors to changes in labour productivity and efficiency in the economy . . . is usually presented in purely qualitative terms. It appears that up to now their contribution has been potential rather than actual. (Eco-nomic Commission for Europe, 1978, p. 77, note 8)

It will be the task of the next chapter to analyse the reasons for this failure of actualisation.

3   THE REFORMS AND WHY THEY FAILED

The 'Pre-reforms'

Having given Khrushchev credit for perceiving the unfavourable trend in capital productivity in the late 1950s, and for making the link between that and the organisational problems of the ministerial planning hierarchy, we have to give him rather less credit for his attempted solution. To counter departmentalism and its attendant evils of 'long cross-hauls' (see p. 17), neglect of potential external economies of scale in regional complexes, etc., Khrushchev thought to create a network of regional economic councils (*sovnarkhozy*), thus breaking up the traditional concentration of economic administrative power in Moscow. He was able at the same time to get rid of his political rivals, the so-called 'anti-Party Group', whose power base was located in the ministerial structure. But nothing was done to modify the degree of centralisation of the system, the success-indicator regime, etc., so that nothing happened to alleviate the supply problem which had lain behind the autarkical tendencies of the ministries. It came as no surprise, then, when the evils of departmentalism were simply replaced by the canker of localism.

If anything, indeed, the *sovnarkhozy* turned out to be even more mischievously autarkic than the ministries had been. Because of the political dimension of the reform, with Khrushchev anxious to reward his own supporters amongst the regionally organised Communist Party hierarchy as well as to squash his rivals, the *sovnarkhozy* were made coterminous with the existing network of politico-administrative republics, provinces, etc. This increased the power and prestige of the local Party apparatus men, but it had three economically deleterious effects. Firstly, it meant that the *sovnarkhozy* were too small — there were originally over a hundred of them. Secondly, it meant that their boundaries had in most cases no economic rationale. Taken together, those two characteristics meant that the 'natural' degree of autarky of the *sovnarkhozy* was in most cases very low, so that the autarkical tendencies were that much more damaging, while the scope for 'rational complex development' was severely limited. In addition, the fact that many Soviet administrative subdivisions are ethnically based allowed an element of sheer local nationalism to enter in and exacerbate localistic tendencies. This was particularly marked in Central Asia, where each of the four union republics was given its own *sovnarkhoz* (Dyker, 1983a, especially Ch. 6).

Khrushchev may also have hoped that the regionalisation of the intermediate planning hierarchy might lessen the degree of *raspylenie sredstv* — of excessive spread of investment resources. If so, he was to be disappointed — that problem too seemed to get worse under the *sovnarkhozy*, partly because of difficulties with the regionalisation of the building industry, partly because the intensely autarkical tendencies of the *sovnarkhozy* ultimately made the supply situation even worse, certainly as far as investment supplies were concerned. Khrushchev's first attempt at reform was, then, a total failure, and by 1962 the *sovnarkhozy* had been largely emasculated, though they were not officially abolished until Kosygin reinstated the ministerial system as part of his 1965 planning reform.

It is odd that Khrushchev continued through the early 1960s to play 'bureaucratic musical chairs' with the creation of all sorts of new central and regional planning bodies which simply further confused an already unwieldy structure. At the same time he has to take some credit for starting the process of reappraisal of the basic element in plan implementation, the success-indicator regime, a process which was to continue throughout the late 1960s and early 1970s. In 1959 he tried the most obvious approach to the problem of making the system more cost-conscious — he introduced cost reduction as an explicit key indicator, having equal status with gross output. Of course, this did not work. Enterprises quickly discovered that with a captive market the easiest way to cut costs is to skimp on materials and quality. But the lesson was learned that any basically physical planning indicator is bound to induce concentration on some dimensions of the production/realisation cycle to the neglect of others. With limited and clear-cut priorities and abundant resources this could almost be an advantage, but as the strategic emphasis moved more in the direction of balanced growth and the resource availability situation tightened, so the need to evolve some kind of synthetic indicator, which would reflect all key aspects of that cycle, intensified. This is the background to the emergence of the notion that the success-indicator the Soviet economy needed was *profit*.

Yevsei Liberman published his classic article 'The plan, profits and bonuses' in *Pravda* in 1962 (Liberman, 1962). The article was important as a political signal that the profit-based reform idea was on, rather than in terms of its specific content, which was diplomatically vague. But we can perceive three main threads in the thinking of the reforming economists of the early 1960s in relation to profit. First, but not necessarily most important, there was the notion of profit as an indicator of the optimal static allocation of resources. Secondly, there was the more dynamic, more X-efficiency-orientated idea that use of profit as a success-indicator would push producing units in the direction of more rapid technical change and higher quality standards. Thus both the cost and quality/specification weaknesses of the gross output indicator would be avoided. Thirdly, there was a purely organisational argument in favour of profit, inasmuch as it could be used not only as a success-indicator, but also as a direct source of incentive payments, which of course gross output never could. Implicit in all this was the idea that planning in general would become more *parametric*, i.e. based more on coefficients which are 'constant in the case under consideration but which may vary from case to case' (Bullock and Stallybrass, 1977, p. 455), whether they be prices, bonus coefficients, plough-back ratios or whatever; in a word, Liberman's approach was ultimately based on the notion of *stable norms*.

In 1963 a pilot scheme was set up in the Bol'shevichka and Mayak textile enterprises involving use of profit as a success-indicator, and with some degree of freedom of price formation, and possibly also some contract flexibility, conceded to enterprises. The pilot scheme was subsequently extended to other enterprises, but its usefulness was limited by the fact that reformed enterprises still had to operate in a largely unreformed environment. In any case, the experiment was quickly overtaken by political events, with Khrushchev falling from power in September 1964, to be replaced by a 'collective leadership' led by Leonid Brezhnev as Party boss and Andrei Kosygin as prime minister, i.e. effectively super-minister for industry. But however much of a break this may have signified in terms of political style, as the new leadership took pains to dissociate itself from Khrushchev's 'harebrained schemes', there was a very substantial degree of continuity on the planning reform dimension. When Kosygin announced his comprehensive planning decree in September 1965, it did, indeed, appear as if the Bol'shevichka/Mayak experiment was simply to be extended throughout the Soviet industry.

The 1965 Planning Reform

The main elements in the reform were as follows:

(1) The total number of planned indicators for the enterprise was to be cut from around 30 to 7 — sales, rate of profit on capital, level of profit, wages fund, basic assortment, payments to and from the state budget, and centralised investment. The first three of these were designed as key indicators, determining bonuses, etc. The norm would be a combination of sales and rate of profit, with sales being replaced by level of profit for some enterprises. Other permutations were subsequently introduced, but not such as to represent any serious modification of the system. Profit was thus well and truly established as a keystone of the planning system, but with a modified output indicator — in the form of sales — sharing pride of place. *A priori*, this seemed a theoretically sound and pragmatically sensible combination.

(2) The incentive system was revamped. There would now be three funds: the material incentive fund, which would pay bonuses to managerial and shop-floor workers alike; the socio-cultural and housing fund; and the production development fund, to finance decentralised investment. The last of these we will come back to under heading (5). The socio-cultural and housing fund was an important innovation, because of the key incentive effect of housing provision in an environment characterised by shortage of accommodation. The material incentive fund gave the enterprise a formally constituted bonus fund of its own for the first time — previously, as we saw earlier, managerial bonuses had come from ministerial funds, while line workers' had been paid out of the wages fund. The wages fund would continue to be one source of shop-floor incentives, but the emphasis would shift to the new fund. The general weight of bonus payments in relation to total remuneration was increased. The scope for earning bonuses increased for everyone, but proportionately more for managerial workers, though overall average differentials between managerial and line workers decreased somewhat between 1965 and 1973 (Yanowitch, 1977, p. 30). The whole system was to be based on stable norms.

(3) A reform of the price system was set in motion, to be completed by 1968. The old price system, with its great and often arbitrary variations in margins over costs and high incidence of 'planned loss-makers', was quite unsuitable for a success-indicator system in which profit played a large part. There was some movement towards scarcity pricing in the area of factor pricing, with the introduction of a standard capital

charge on all industrial fixed capital on which loan interest was not being paid. The charge was, however, set at the very low level of 6 per cent. Some limited forms of rental payment were introduced in the extractive industries (Fedorenko, 1968), but these fell far short of a generalised system of payment for the use of unique natural advantages. As far as wholesale and retail prices are concerned, the aim of the reform was simply to establish some kind of uniformity in profit rates between different sectors and enterprises. It was, in fact, very much a cost-plus price reform, based on a kind of modified ratchet principle. It succeeded in ironing out a good proportion of the anomalies of the old system but left light industry with systematically higher profit rates than heavy, and permitted the survival of a good deal of planned loss-making − inevitably, since no generalised land rent structure had been introduced.

(4) The system of finance for centralised investment was to be moved away from its traditionally almost exclusive reliance on the non-returnable budgetary grant. Retained profits and bank credit were programmed to develop as major alternative forms of finance for fixed capital investment. Despite the establishment of almost ludicrously low rates of interest, originally as little as 0.5 per cent, bank credit did not take off in its new role, perhaps because the new price structure gave many enterprises such high gross profit margins that plough-backs were just too easy. By 1972 only 33.8 per cent of total centralised investment in Soviet industry was being financed from the budget, with as much as 60.0 per cent being funded from retentions. Bank credit accounted for just 6.2 per cent of the total in that year (Pessel', 1977, p. 51).

(5) There was to be a limited marketisation/decentralisation of the system in relation to some minor subsectors of the economy. With the creation of the production and development fund, the importance of decentralised investment increased sharply, and by 1972 it was accounting for nearly 20 per cent of total state investment (Solomin, 1977, p. 62). While the introduction of the possibility of financing centralised investment from profits represented in essence no more than an accounting change, the planning of decentralised investment projects was to be strictly the preserve of the enterprise management, subject to planned limits for aggregate decentralised investment. Would-be decentralised investors were permitted to place special orders for investment supplies with other enterprises on the basis of a new enterprise statute which established the right of primary producing units:

to accept orders from other enterprises and organisations for above-plan production on the basis of materials supplied by the client, or using own materials and waste products – on condition that this is not to the detriment of the fulfilment of the state plan and obligations according to agreements. (Bodashevskii, 1968)

There would be a new flexibility in supply arrangements for a number of basic commodity categories. A provision whereby certain oil products, construction materials and chemicals could be obtained at *snabsbyty* (supply depots) without the classical *naryad* (allocation certificate) was introduced in certain areas in 1966 ('Sistema material' no-tekhnicheskogo snabzheniya', 1969). The 'supply on the basis of orders' (*snabzhenie po zakazam*) system in the construction sector was experimentally introduced in 1970, and is presumably a development of non-allocational supply for the building industry (Chernyavskii, 1976). A decree passed in 1969 provided for the transfer of whole enterprises on to non-allocational supply in certain cases. But dispensing with the *naryad* was an essentially limited step, probably removing a form-filling irritation rather than revolutionising the supply system. Non-allocational supply involves no freedom of price formation, and may involve little effective freedom of contract, as it is not clear to what extent enterprises may be permitted to 'shop around' among *snabsbyty* in different areas.

A more radical departure was the creation of a network of wholesale shops to ply small-scale wholesale (*melkooptovyi*) trade. Wholesale shops operate largely without any kind of constraint in terms of how much of what they may supply to whom. As of 1969 just 30 per cent of the turnover of these shops was subject to 'limits', whereby ministries retain quantitative control over allocations of key commodities to particular shops, though enterprises still do not require formal *naryady*. Since then the proportion of the total turnover of the shops subject to limits may have risen to around two-thirds (Rabinovich, 1976, pp. 169, 219). Small-scale wholesale shops are primarily concerned with selling goods in small batches. There seems to be virtually complete freedom of contract here, subject to plan targets for total turnover, but wholesale shops do not appear to be allowed to fix their own prices. The 1965 reform also created the category of 'wholesale fairs' (*yarmarki*) as one-off occasions to bring prospective suppliers and buyers of 'bits and pieces' together, and these must be permitted a degree of freedom of price formation to function at all. Commission shops, which basically exist to permit private individuals to sell off unwanted goods, but which are systematically used for procurement purposes by the R and D establishment, are subject only to the constraint that goods cannot be sold at a price higher than that of the same commodity in a state shop (Katsenelinboigen, 1978, p. 174).

The distinctions between these various categories of more flexible supply arrangements have in practice been less than clear, so that it is difficult to be sure about the coverage of published figures on the volume of transactions they involve. In 1965 the total turnover of wholesale-trading organisations (which may or may not include non-allocational supply) was just 70 million rubles, and by 1968 it had grown to 583 million rubles, with an expected figure of 885 million rubles by 1969 – about 0.3 per cent of Soviet national income in that year ('Sistema material' no-tekhnicheskogo snabzheniya', 1969). In 1968 small-scale wholesale trade proper accounted for just 0.5 per cent of total supply turnover (Gofman and Petrakov, 1968), but by 1974 wholesale trade as a whole represented 3–5 per cent of total trade (Drogichinskii, 1974, p. 31).

The third major element of limited marketisation introduced into the system in 1965 related to subsidiary industrial activity in the countryside, a key subsector in the context of the seasonality of much agricultural work and the poverty of urban-industrial supplies to the countryside. It was the 1967 decree on agriculture that spelt out the new regime in this connection, and though the exact extent of auto-nomisation of subsidiary industrial activity was left a little unclear, a legal source from 1973 states that

> *kolkhozy, sovkhozy* and other agricultural enterprises, and inter-*kolkhoz* organisations, sell the output of subsidiary enterprises and workshops on the basis of agreements concluded with the state trading network, industrial enterprises, consumer cooperatives, and other economic organisations. *Prices and technical production specifications are agreed on by the parties concerned* [emphasis added]. There is an established procedure for supplying subsidiary enterprises with the necessary materials, equipment and credit. (Lur'e, 1973, p. 23)

This suggests that the only specific constraint imposed on these kinds of economic activity should be through the retention of some degree of central control over the supply (to the subsidiary enterprise) and credit sides. Gosbank does, in fact, extend six-year loans to *sovkhoz* and inter-*kolkhoz* organisations, though not to *kolkhozy* as such, for the construction of subsidiary enterprises (Pronin, 1969, p. 47). On the other hand, mushroom gathering seems to be subject to strict quotas and procurement prices (Barsukov, 1971, p. 7), and the general rule that subsidiary industrial activity should never be to the detriment of basic agricultural activities meant that the central authorities retained substantial powers of occasional interference.

Subsidiary industrial activity in the countryside, covering canning and processing, building materials production, construction itself, timber and textiles, was worth 4.7 billion rubles in 1966 (Gusev, 1970, p. 6), and 8.5 billion rubles in 1970 (Gusev, 1971, p. 7) – almost three per cent of Soviet national income in that year. In some regions it accounted for 50 per cent of *kolkhoz* income from sales in 1970 (Utochkin and Kuznetsov, 1970, p. 95).

(6) The reform decree also predicated a new emphasis on 'direct links' between enterprises, without explaining, even in general terms, what this was to mean. The radical interpretation of direct links, which was espoused by the 'marketing' faction of the Soviet economics profession at the time, saw it as a complement to the development of more flexible supply arrangements, an aspect of a comprehensive transition to 'state wholesale trading' as the basis of the planning system. In this reading, direct links would certainly involve some generalised freedom of contract, and perhaps also some freedom in the price-fixing domain. In the conservative interpretation of direct links, by contrast, enterprises with established supply links would simply come together to work out, and commit themselves to, details of specification and assortment: no extra freedom in relation to the basic contract or the prices at which deliveries are invoiced would necessarily be implied.

(7) Although the ministerial system was re-established, the centre sought to limit the redepartmentalisation of the supply system – no doubt with the possible resurgence of autarkical patterns in mind – by creating a national network of supply depots under the aegis of a new body called Gossnab – State Supply Committee. (A committee of the same name had existed before 1953.) Gossnab would do the bulk of the detailed Material Balance work at the plan compilation stage, leaving Gosplan to concentrate on the 'commanding heights' – that still meant Gosplan handling about 2,000 commodity groups, and Gossnab about 18,000. But through its national network Gossnab would also supervise the actual *consignment* of planned deliveries.

(8) As we said earlier, the new profit success-indicator was clearly expected to strengthen the incentive to innovation at the shop-floor

level. But in 1969 a follow-up decree established special prices and bonus schemes to stimulate the introduction of new products.

(9) Another follow-up decree of 1969 recommended the extension of an experiment which had been going on for two years at the Shchekino Chemical Combine (Tula province). The essence of this experiment was simple enough – managers were given the right to make workers redundant, though they were supposed to help them find new work, and use part of the funds thus released to increase incentive payments to the rest of the work-force. This gave concrete expression to some vague statements from 1965 about increasing managerial rights in the personnel area. Traditionally, Soviet directors had had very limited powers of dismissal, and though this did not stop individual directors taking the law into their own hands on occasion, it did create a level of job security virtually unknown for blue-collar workers in the West. This helps us to understand how the kind of easy-going work practices we mentioned in the last chapter could survive, and it did, of course, all fit in quite nicely with the extensive employment patterns characterising Stalinist development strategy. But by the same token a Soviet government increasingly forced to look to the labour productivity variable for prospects of future growth was bound to wonder whether they could go on affording a tenured work-force. In 1971, 121 enterprises were on the Shchekino system, and by 1975 the chemicals industry had been largely transferred on to the experiment, though Shchekino-system enterprises still employed only 3 per cent of the total labour force in that year (Dyker, 1981a, p. 58).

Preoccupation with the problem of efficient allocation and utilisation of the work-force showed up also in the development, from 1966, of a network of employment offices (*sluzhba truda*) under the aegis of republican committees for labour resource utilisation. This represented the first systematic approach to the problem of labour-placement (*trudoustroistvo*) since the abolition of the old labour exchanges in the early 1930s, and by 1970 *sluzhba truda* were processing more than a million workers annually in the RSFSR (accounting for about half the population of the USSR) alone. Labour placement has remained basically a republican matter, although the republican committees for labour resource utilisation were subordinated to a reorganised All-Union State Committee for Labour and Social Problems (Goskomtrud) in 1977 (Dyker, 1981a, p. 43).

The 1965 Planning Reform in Retrospect

In a constantly changing world the assessment of economic policy measures is notoriously difficult, but we can start off here by looking back at Table 2.4, and reminding ourselves that the fillip to Soviet economic growth in the late 1960s was primarily associated with an improvement in the capital productivity situation – to the extent at least that the continued downward trend in that variable proceeded substantially more slowly than it had been doing. Micro-economic analysis confirms that the introduction of the capital charge (at too low a level or not), and the institution of rate of profit on capital as a key success-indicator, did induce enterprise managers to unload large volumes of excess equipment – of course under the old system 'hoarding' was costless, and could pay big dividends because it gave pushers something they could swap when trying to solve supply problems (Schroeder, 1968).

But the failure of the reform to do anything to the rate of growth of labour productivity, in an era before rising primary material costs had really started to bite, suggests a failure to engineer the desired 'change of gear', a failure to make an effective transition from extensive to intensive development. Certainly we have to be careful about judging the effect of the reform in crudely quantitative terms. Good weather and good harvests in a number of years in the late 1960s provided a fillip to aggregate growth rates which had nothing to do with planning reforms, inside or outside agriculture. In any case the quality problem had been a major issue in the discussion leading up to the reform, and travellers' reports from the Soviet Union in the immediate post-reform period suggest that there was some general improvement in quality, while trends in exports of the more sophisticated types of goods showed Soviet industry in a fairly good light. But complaints in the Soviet press about quality problems of the traditional type, to the extent of track suits with different lengths of arms and legs, were as frequent after 1965 as before – no doubt partly because the authorities were increasingly concerned about the problem (Dyker, 1976, pp. 62-3). And of course precisely because of the increasing complexity and technical sophistication of the economy, these problems tended more and more to hamper industry itself. The supply situation in relation to spare parts remained critical, despite the wholesale shops, and the incidence of pushing, if anything, actually increased:

'Pushers' . . . continue to perfect their 'weapons'. And it seems to me that their activity has intensified in recent times. Managers took to the new arrangements on supplies with alacrity . . . And suddenly, after all this, it turns out that there are more 'pushers' than ever, for all your 'economic levers' . . . A contradiction? Certainly, and it makes you think. (Ryzhov, 1972, p. 3)

We shall return to the interpretation of that contradiction later on.

No less suggestive in terms of the underlying supply problem is the fact that, despite the creation of the Gossnab system, departmentalist autarkical tendencies reasserted themselves in the years after 1965 with extraordinary vigour. In the period 1965-9 the number of building and building-maintenance organisations in the city of Odessa grew four times, with all the new ones being under different departments (Koppel' and Brig, 1969). Other sources from around that time emphasised continuing supply uncertainty as a major reason for the survival of *shturmovshchina* into the new system (Dyker, 1976, pp. 63-4). Marginal improvements there may, then, have been, but all the characteristic efficiency problems of the traditional system seem to have carried over into the new. To find out why, we have to look more closely at the provisions of the Kosygin reform.

Perhaps the most striking feature of the 1965 provisions was that they involved *virtually no overall decentralisation* of the system. The reduction in the total number of planning indicators sent down to the enterprise represented only a formal decentralisation − in practice it had, of course, always been beyond the capabilities of the planning hierarchy to ensure consistency between 20 or 30 indicators, and that is precisely one of the reasons why in practice gross output tended to have an almost unique priority. Cutting down the total number of planning indicators removed an irritation from the life of the Soviet manager, but in terms of the key indicators which determined bonuses, promotion, etc. *the situation actually became more complex.* The central authorities continued to try to plan production assortment at enterprise level in considerable detail, and if we look at the number of commodity groups planned centrally, we find that it fell from *c.* 20,000 in the late 1960s to around 15,500 in 1977 ('Problemy razrabotki . . .', 1977, p. 115). In computational terms this is not a significant change. Despite the increasing availability of computers, the technology of Soviet plan construction had consequently changed strikingly little by the mid-1970s:

Each year Gosplan USSR works out some hundreds of material
balances by product types, and a great deal of experience has been
accumulated in this field. Inter-product and inter-sectoral balances,
which can provide a greater degree of consistency between the
production and allocation of goods in interlinked sectors, are less
widely used. In the organs of Gossnab USSR balancing has still not
been widely developed as a basis for the production of material-
technical supply plans. (Rabinovich, 1976, p. 214)

The various elements of partial decentralisation discussed under heading
(5) above were of course not substantial enough to affect the overall
level of centralisation, whatever their potential 'qualitative' significance.
And the tradition of administrative control over prices was recon-
secrated in the price reform of 1966-7 to such a degree that even
wholesale shops and the like were probably given very little freedom
in this domain. Under the original provisions, the formation and dis-
bursement of bonus funds were to be on the basis of rules which left
a good deal of freedom to the enterprise. But by 1971 changes were
being introduced which reasserted the right of ministries to modify
bonus rules.

The transition to profit as a key success-indicator implied a degree
of transition to a more parametric system, to a system just as centralised, perhaps, but less directly centralised. In fact, the Soviet planners
did, under the reform, insist on *setting targets* for profit. It is difficult
to see any good reason for this – rather it smacks of the obstinacy of
the old habits of command. But with sales targets being imposed as
well, for perfectly good reasons we must add, the command principle
was clearly much less modified at the general level than it might have
been. It was modified very significantly in the peripheral areas of
radical marketisation, but once again we have to say that even in potential terms this was very small beer. Procedures have, certainly, been
introduced into R and D planning whereby special price differentials
and coefficients tie bonuses directly to the return on innovations
(Cooper, 1979). As we shall see in Chapter 5, similar approaches have
been tried out experimentally in construction. Thus movement away
from the command principle has tended to affect specific sectors or
subsectors, rather than the planning system as a whole. As far as enterprises are concerned, the classic principle that they be *instructed* how
much of what to produce or realise, from whom to obtain their inputs,
and to whom to send their outputs, remained largely untouched.

How did all this affect the actual operation of the new success-indicators? Let us take sales first. It is not clear, in a situation where customer enterprise cannot argue about prices or change suppliers, that a switch from output to sales as key output-based indicator will make a great deal of difference. One can easily find cases from the post-reform period where badly substandard consumer goods have simply been sent back to the producer (see Dyker, 1976, p. 63), and under the new success-indicator this does mean automatic loss of bonuses. But of course even under the old system managers who pushed their luck too far on the quality side tended to run into *political* sanctions – hence the indignant articles in *Pravda* from which we learn so much. More important is what happens when deliveries from one industrial enterprise to another are substandard, or inaccurately specified, without being totally useless. The trouble with sending the whole lot back is that this will almost certainly mean that the manager will fail to fulfil the monthly or quarterly plan, thus breaking golden rule No. 1 of the Soviet executive bent on survival. And if, under the pressure of the given enterprise's own plans, a substandard consignment is wholly or partly used, the right to sue the supplier is forfeited under Soviet commercial law (Vlasov, 1984). Even if specification is so far out that the supplies cannot be used, they can, of course, always be hoarded with a view to disposing of them through the pusher network on which the manager is in any case the more dependent, the more often mis-specified deliveries are received. While the 1965 planning reform introduced a significant sanction on the hoarding of capital goods, it did not materially alter the situation with respect to supplies in general.

In a market economy clients initially respond to quality and specification problems by demanding price discounts, or making threatening noises about changing supplier in the future. The problem in the Soviet case, with the introduction of a sales success-indicator not backed up by substantial decentralisation or relaxation of the command principle, is that the ultimate sanction was the only one available; no basis whatsoever was created for the development of any regularised process of continuous adjustment in the matching of supplies and demands.

We can say exactly the same things about the introduction of profit as a success-indicator. With fixed prices and captive customers a supplier can improve the profit position by skimping, or using shoddy materials, just as he can the position with a straight cost-reduction indicator. With hundreds of thousands of prices to be fixed by the State Committee for Prices, it is unavoidable that there will be inconsistencies in the profitability of individual items. Bonus-maximising managers will be able to increase profits by distorting assortment towards product lines carrying higher profit margins, and once again the client enterprise will be prevented by the rigidity of the price and contract system from making any kind of flexible response. Under the 1965 provisions the authorities *sought* to retain direct control over assortment — they were not looking to the profit success-indicator to do the job for them. But because general over-centralisation prevented them from exercising that control effectively, a vacuum was created which the profit success-indicator was prevented from filling by continued restrictions in the price and contract area. If, of course, an expected consignment simply does not turn up at all, there is *absolutely* nothing an enterprise in a Soviet-type system can do, whatever the success-indicator regime, except resort to political string-pulling and the pusher network.

There were other problems with the profit-based indicators. The combination of cost-plus pricing, failure to institute a proper profit-maximising rule, and failure to permit any sharp increase in the degree to which resource flows were permitted to respond to price/profit signals meant that profit was largely unable to function in its allocative role. To the extent that it was, it may have tended to misallocation rather than allocation. *Rate* of profit did reinforce the capital-dishoarding effect of the capital charge. But it was a peculiarly unsuitable indicator to introduce at a time when enterprises were being brought more into the investment decision-making process. Clearly an enterprise which has, for any reason, an above-average gross rate of profit on existing capital stock will be discouraged by this indicator from undertaking any new investment which would pull that average down, irrespective of its net present value. The failure of the price reform to iron out historical anomalies in sectoral profit rates made this problem that much more serious (Liberman, 1968, pp. 54–5; Bunich, 1967, p. 47).

To sum up, then, profit in the given context earns just about zero marks in relation to resource allocation. It was prevented by the continued rigidity of the price and contract set-up from making anything like its potential contribution in terms of general X-efficiency problems. It did, however, work perfectly well as a basis for financing enterprise funds.

The second major specific difficulty with the 1965 reform related to the position of intermediate planning bodies. As we noted in Chapter 1, the traditional planning system was remarkably simple in terms of how the line of command operated. The centre dished out aggregate output targets to the ministries and main administrations, and they broke them down into specific targets for producing units. Ministerial workers were not on bonus schemes as such, but in more general terms their prospects depended on performance in relation to plan just as much as those of enterprise managements. Plan fulfilment, in a word, meant exactly the same thing for everyone, from Gosplan planners down to shop-floor workers. The 1965 reform changed all that. Ministries, etc. would remain, or rather be re-established, as essentially administrative bodies, receiving aggregate instructions from Gosplan in terms of gross output. This stood to reason, because sales contracts were imposed on enterprises, not ministries. It did, however, create a problem of 'translating' output targets into sales targets, and it is hardly surprising that in the early days of the reform the ministries were frequently accused of setting unofficial gross output targets for their enterprises.

But the problem went deeper than that. Now that enterprises in various ways 'paid' for their capital stock as they had never done before, what happens if a ministry or *glavk* decides to transfer equipment from one enterprise to another? Should this be forbidden, or should compensation be paid when it does occur? More generally, the fact that intermediate planning bodies were not on *khozraschet* (business accounting) like their subordinate enterprises meant (a) that they did not have formally constituted profit-and-loss accounts and incentive funds; (b) that they were not juridical persons, so that enterprises had no basis for litigation against them if they acted in a way detrimental to the local interests of the enterprise. Under the new system, with enterprises constrained to place much more emphasis on financial flows, this emerged as a serious problem.

The approach of the Brezhnev/Kosygin government to that problem was to try to push the *khozraschet* principle further up the planning heirarchy. By the late 1960s one ministry — the Ministry for Instrument-Making — was already on a regime involving 'elements of *khozraschet*', though this does not appear to have meant much more than 100 per cent self-financing of centralised investment in the sector. Experiments with ministerial *khozraschet* continued into the mid-1970s, but more substantial progress was made at the level between ministry and enterprise. During the early reform period a number of *glavki* were put on *khozraschet*, but that approach was superseded with the decree on associations (*ob"edinenie*), published in 1973. This created a highly complex system at the sub-intermediate level, in which the norm was for so-called *production associations* to group together fairly small numbers of associated enterprises, with the latter sometimes but not always losing their juridicial independence, and *industrial associations* taking over the role of the old *glavki*. Production associations are always on full *khozraschet*, and there appear to be substantial elements of *khozraschet* at industrial association level. But the *ob"edinenie* reform has at best shifted the incidence of the problem of dovetailing administration and the post-reform interpretation of *khozraschet* to a higher instance (Dyker, 1983a, p. 34). Indeed clashes between ministry and association are surely inevitable as long as the former are forced to work with a system still plagued by supply uncertainty, and still containing substantial elements of tautness. In such an environment they could hardly be expected to ensure plan fulfilment without recourse to their traditional ploys of chopping and changing plan targets for subordinates, shifting around resources, etc.

The association reform was not only about the balance of administration and *khozraschet*. Recognising that the general measures of 1965 had not resulted in any dramatic improvement in the supply situation, and that in this context it was going to be very difficult to control organisational-autarkical tendencies, the authorities sought through the establishment of production associations to create rationalised combinations of main-activity and ancillary enterprises, which would at least cut the cost, in terms of transport and excess capacity, of organisational autarky. They do not appear to have been particularly successful in this (Golub', 1974), no doubt partly because it was left to the ministries to do the rationalising. Finally, the Soviet leadership saw in the 1973 decree a basis for improving the innovation performance of the Soviet economy. This statement in itself implies that the approach to the innovation problem embodied in the decrees of 1965 and 1969 had not worked. Let us investigate that proposition.

Just as profit with fixed prices and contracts may not in practice stimulate high quality and the study of clients' needs, so it may not necessarily create effective incentives to innovation. With sales targets to be fulfilled, furthermore, and the ratchet principle still very much alive (see discussion below), enterprise managers may be sceptical about innovation even when it is likely to improve profit performance. In any case, none of this has any effect on the flow of R and D from research institutes to producing units in the first place. The 1969 decree did little apropos the latter problem, except to instruct the institutes to mend their ways. In relation to the former, its reliance on special prices and bonuses for innovations ran into two types of difficulty. First, the special price system was over-complex and badly designed, so that enterprises might often be stimulated to do the wrong thing (Lavelle, 1974). Secondly, there is the problem of simulation. The easy way to earn special innovation bonuses is through 'innovation' rather than innovation. The more sophisticated an economy becomes, the more emphasis it places on consumer goods, the greater the scope for such simulation becomes. By giving associations their own R and D facilities (some special mixed 'scientific-production associations' were also created) the authorities obviously hoped to speed up the process of communication from research team to production unit. They seem also to have believed that the association would be in a position to take a longer view on the merits of innovation. In practice, continued 'petty tutelage' over the new sub-intermediate bodies ensured that their view on this could not be very different from that of an enterprise (see Zakharov and Petrov, 1974).

Perhaps the most significant failure of the Kosygin reform was in relation to limited liberalisation in specific subsectors. Let us start by looking at decentralised investment. The first thing that happened there was that would-be investors, replete with production-development funds, ran into serious difficulties in getting hold of the physical resources to make their decentralised investment plans reality (Gorushkin, 1969). Giving institutions in a Soviet-type economy funds to finance essentially unplanned activities may run into the problem that other institutions have not been assigned plans to produce the corresponding supplies – hence the importance of the change in the enterprise statute cited earlier. Enterprises, it was hoped, would feel encouraged to produce lines not included in the plan, or to produce extra output on planned production lines, thus improving performance in relation to the profit indicator, though not, presumably, in relation to basic sales and assortment plans.

That this did not happen seems to be largely related to the vigorous survival of the ratchet and modified Micawber principles into the post-reform period (Dyker, 1981b, pp. 127–8). Enterprises had little choice but to remain above all concerned that sales/output plans be fulfilled, and at best indifferent to the production of large-scale over-plan surpluses (Zangurashvili, 1976). They must have remained positively reluctant to *report* any such surpluses, so that unofficial direct disposal would in any case be considered preferable to official. The operation of the ratchet and Micawber factors may have been strengthened in this regard by more general systemic tendencies. To the extent that the planning balance has remained taut, there may not have been, with the best will in the world, much potential surplus around (see Varavka,

1975), while surpluses that were reported were often quickly gobbled up by intermediate planning authorities (Protsenko and Soloveichik, 1976, p. 24). Ministries, still obsessed with minimising a supply problem that had been eased to only a minor degree, proceeded with their traditional autarkic policies to the extent of making it extremely difficult for enterprises to take on extra commitments to 'outsiders'. Cases were even reported of ministries issuing formal regulations obliging subordinate enterprises to give priority to intra-sectoral supply, even in cases where allocation certificates had not been issued by Gossnab (Khashutogov, 1976).

The second thing that happened with decentralised investment, round about 1969/70, was that it began to sort out its supply problems with a vengeance, to the extent that in 1971 the plan for total decentralisation was overfulfilled by 26 per cent, while the plan for centralised investment was underfulfilled by 4 per cent. In 1971 there were no fewer than 880 projects under construction that were outside the plan, but using materials and men earmarked for planned projects ('Vypolnenie plana . . .', 1972, p. 3). It seems clear that enterprise managers, originally baulked by the weakness of formal supply arrangements for decentralised investment, were by the early 1970s turning to the unofficial pusher network to filch supplies away from centralised investment. This helps us to understand the paradox noted earlier of an apparent *increase* in the activity of pushers after the reform.

The development of subsidiary industrial production in the countryside followed a very similar pattern, and for the same ultimate reason. 'The supply to *kolkhozy* of equipment for processing and subsidiary production is not a function of state organisations' (Pozdnyakov, 1968, p. 101). Trading organisations could, on the basis of agreements described as *daval'cheskii*, transfer goods from the 'market fund' to collective and state farms for use as 'raw and ancillary materials' (Pronin, 1969, p. 48). Payment for these deliveries might be made in the form of counterpart consignments of the finished goods. Industrial enterprises were encouraged to sell off surplus machinery, inventory, raw materials and offcuts to agricultural organisations. But many reports indicate only fractional satisfaction of subsidiary industrial supply needs from official allocations. In some cases, e.g. that of timber, it may have been possible to meet the bulk of needs from own supplies and direct supplies from local enterprises (Sokolov, 1969). But even with state farms, which might presumably tend to get better treatment than *kolkhozy*, the acuteness of the problem is underlined by the testimony of a *sovkhoz* director:

Early in the morning I rush off to the *oblast'* centre, 80 kilometres away, abandoning a mass of production affairs. Having spent the day running around construction and supply organisations I return late. The foreman is waiting for me. What about the bricks, the things for the carpenters? He doesn't even bother to ask about roofing felt and glass. (Vasil'ev, 1968, p. 10)

Despite this, agro-industrial operations flourished, partly because they fulfilled very great needs, partly because the freedom of movement conceded them made possible unofficial supply operations on a grand scale. It is reported that 37 per cent of all cases of misappropriation in Odessa *oblast'* in 1971 occurred in the subsector, with a corresponding figure for 1972 of 24 per cent. At one point more than two hundred illegal subsidiary enterprises were operating in the province, many of them created by 'sharpers' (Yasinskii, 1973, p. 19). A legal specialist reports that among the most common forms of unlawful act committed on *kolkhozy* are

deals between collective farms and private go-betweens involving the sale of *kolkhoz* production or the acquisition of materials. Violations of the second type are particularly common, which is largely explicable in terms of deficiencies in the organisation of material-technical supply to *kolkhozy*. (Tarnavskii, 1973, p. 26)

The kinds of problems that decentralised investment and subsidiary industrial activity ran into, and the way these problems were solved, highlight the failure of the various kinds of free trade introduced to take off in a big way, which in turn reflects the failure of the reformed planning system to create effective incentives for the production of special orders. Of course, because sales is a *gross* indicator the new system failed in any case to obviate the traditional disincentive to produce even *planned* quotas of bits and pieces. Most fundamentally, the failure to decentralise meaningfully meant that the planners could not give up the ratchet, which meant that managers could not give up their anti-ratchet ploys. Table 3.1 gives a revealing picture of the operations of an apparently fairly successful wholesale shop in Odessa. The most significant thing to emerge from the table is that the bulk of purchases are coming from the supply network itself, including other free trading organisations. (This means, by the way, that official figures on shop turnover must exaggerate their real importance because of elements of double-counting.) The proportion of total purchases

Table 3.1: Percentage Breakdown of Decentralised Purchases of Material Resources by the Universal Shop under the Odeselektromashsnabsbyt Administration

Decentralised Purchases	Total	Purchases within the Zone of the Administration	Purchases outside the Zone of the Administration
From industrial enterprise	24.6	37.9	17.9
From *snabsbyt* organisations under Gossnab USSR	53.1	4.0	77.2
of which from small-scale wholesale shops	16.9	0.4	25.0
From trade and *snabsbyt* organisations under ministries and departments	22.3	58.1	4.9
Total	100.0	100.0	100.0

Source: Rabinovich, 1976, p. 171.

coming directly from industrial enterprises is fairly low overall, and is even lower in relation to non-local enterprises. Some proportion of purchases from the trading network must represent *indirect* purchases of enterprise surpluses, but the bulk of these must surely reflect 'shunting-around' of planned, but incorrectly despatched, consignments. This confirms the failure of free trading organisations to emerge as powerful instruments for the redistribution of surplus production coming directly from enterprises.

We should certainly not exaggerate the quantitative importance of these elements of autonomisation introduced by Kosygin – around 1970 they probably added up to just about 10 per cent of Soviet national income. *But they graphically illustrate the key principle that a degree of general decentralisation is a necessary condition of more radical autonomisation in particular subsectors, that the 'stable norms' slogan is meaningless in an over-centralised economy.* Just as interesting is the way in which the Soviet authorities reacted when things began to get a little out of hand. Perceiving the ever more vigorous development of the 'second economy' within the industrial supplies field, perceiving the threat to central priorities posed through the under-mining of centralised investment plans by decentralised, the leadership decided on a sharp clamp-down. In 1973 the overfulfilment of de-centralised investment plans was banned (Isaev, 1973, p. 32). By 1975 decentralised investment had fallen to 15 per cent of total state invest-ment (Gribov, 1976, p. 88), while production development funds were already by that year being commonly used to finance centralised investment (Dementsev, 1975). By 1976 it had become 'a pure formality that investments implemented on the basis of the production development fund . . . are called decentralised' (Pessel', 1976, p. 56). The early 1970s saw a powerful government impetus towards the creation of inter-*kolkhoz* and mixed *sovkhoz-kolkhoz* associations, involving agricultural activity and subsidiary industrial operations. As far as the latter are concerned, there has been a considerable degree of variation in the specific planning arrangements involved (see Dyker, 1981b, pp. 140-1), but it is clear that the general tenor of the new arrangements was to deprive the subsidiary industrial subsector of its autonomy. 'The progressive transformation of associations into basic *khozraschet* links leads to a reduction in the number of production units, brings them closer to the central state organs of administration, and makes it possible to improve the centralised management of their activity' (Ekonomicheskie Problemy . . ., 1976, p. 278). As far as free trade is concerned, of course, development was never so vigorous as to raise the issue of reassertion of control.

Going through the Motions: the Brezhnev Ascendancy

Though never officially repealed, and to this day the formal framework within which Soviet planning proceeds, the Kosygin reform in a sense dies at some point in the early 1970s. To understand why, we have to look more closely at the political economy of the reform process. Up until 1968 the more uncompromising marketisers among the reformists were still hoping for a decisive move in the direction of market socialism through a radical interpretation of direct links. This would obviously directly facilitate the development of wholesale trade, but it would also do so indirectly — by permitting substantial decentralisation, and therefore leaving the ratchet principle largely redundant. Political developments in 1967 and 1968 put an end to this hope.

The economic and political reforms in Czechoslovakia, culminating in the Prague Spring and the Soviet invasion in August 1968, alerted the Soviet establishment to the general political dangers of allowing too much economic reform. (In Hungary Kadar's power and prestige permitted the introduction of a New Economic Model that was as low-profile on the political side as it was radical on the economic.) More specifically, the professional Party apparatus — the city and provincial Party secretaries, etc. — read a lesson which was, indeed, already there to be read from the Yugoslav experience. In a creaky, over-centralised system, the Party apparatus man has a key trouble-shooting role to play — a role which because of the dominance of supply problems in everyday production life tends to reduce to that of a kind of super-pusher. Without actually being on formal success-indicator regimes, local Party secretaries are judged by the economic success of their parishes in much the same way as managers and ministerial administrators. To ensure that success, *apparatchiki* must make systematic use of political influence and cajolery to keep supply lines open. This makes for a hectic life, but it also gives a powerful political group a strong vested interest in the *very weaknesses* of the traditional planning system. The more successful is economic reform, the more the *apparatchik* finds himself out of a job, as became evident in Czechoslovakia as early as 1967 (Urbanek, 1968). Just as Brezhnev, with his impeccable apparatus background, was establishing his political ascendancy, so it became clear that, whatever this round of Soviet economic reform was to mean, it was not to mean the dismantling of physical allocation of industrial supplies.

But as we have seen in relation to decentralised investment, agro-industrial activity, etc., it was inevitable once that decision had been taken, that the elements of autonomisation which survived the 1968 reaction should come into direct conflict with the *dirigiste* planning still prevalent in the rest of the economy. It is perfectly understandable that the leadership and apparatus could not tolerate the threat to state priorities posed by decentralised investment in the early 1970s, could not tolerate the mushrooming of the 'grey' economy in the country-side. Given their political preconceptions and perception of self-interest, it is hardly surprising that they interpreted the paradoxes of those developments as proof that market socialism does not work, rather than as proof that market socialism cannot work unless you give it a chance. As we saw earlier, one can make exactly the same point about use of profit as a success-indicator. We should not be surprised if the establishment interpretation was that the failure of profit in that role in the late 1960s and 1970s was evidence of its inherent weaknesses, rather than of the inappropriateness of the medium in which it was asked to operate.

The fourfold increase in world oil and gold prices at the end of 1973, representing the culmination of a process of realignment of primary material prices which had, for instance, already seen timber prices rise by several hundred per cent, introduced a new dimension into the situation. With much-enhanced hard currency purchasing power, Brezhnev seems to have thought that increased imports of

Western technology would be an adequate substitute for sustained economic reform (Kaser, 1975, pp. 204–5). Soviet imports of machinery and equipment from the West increased 96 per cent between 1974 and 1975 (Economic Commission for Europe, 1977a, p. 103). Thus political preferences, the organisational implications of the same, and the *deux ex machina* of the oil crisis conspired to bring an end to the first major impetus to planning reform in the Soviet Union. The 1970s witnessed a progressive de-emphasis of profit as a success-indicator, and a tendency to return to the use of simple, as opposed to synthetic, indicators. At the same time the role of profits as a source of enterprise finance was if anything somewhat enhanced, and this reflected an on-going concern to make the planning system, still essentially a centralised command system, more sensitive to costs, and to rates of value-added. Indeed the mid-1970s saw the development of a new success-indicator which focused on *net* output in a way that no standard Soviet indicator had ever done.

The obvious virtue of a value-added success-indicator is that it avoids the tendency to induce excessive buying-in of materials, excessive bulk, neglect of components, etc. built in to *any* gross indicator, be it gross output or sales. The drawback to crude net output indicators is that they tend to induce precisely the opposite distortion – excessive in-plant processing, as the Soviet planners found from experiments carried on at the time of Khrushchev (see Nove, 1961, p. 159). The clever thing about the new indicator of the 1970s – normed net output (*normativnaya chistaya produktsiya*), hereafter NNO – is that it obviates this problem. NNO is calculated on the basis of sector- or product-based norms for the relationship of net output, defined as wage costs + profit, to total sales. Thus in principle, and as long as the ratchet is not around, an enterprise which effects a given level of sales with a less-than-normal level of wage expenditure will improve its profit, and hence its fund-forming position, while still fulfilling its NNO target. The enterprise does, in fact, have an incentive to minimise unit processing costs, subject to the fulfilment of the NNO target (Rogin, 1979).

NNO was developed with the problem of measuring labour productivity particularly in mind, so that its relationship to the general strategic issues facing the Brezhnev government need hardly be spelt out. It involves a number of fairly familiar implementational problems: as long as prices and contracts are fixed, enterprise can simulate good NNO performance just as they can good profit performance; as long as NNO is calculated on the basis of sales, which in the given context is not very different from gross output, then any distortions in the reporting or indeed the execution of that planned task will be reflected in the reported level of NNO (Hanson, 1983). More fundamentally, any advantages that the new indicator has are surely more than cancelled out by the enormous number of calculations it imposes on already overworked planners. The more highly aggregated the NNO coefficients, the more scope there is for enterprise to spot and concentrate on product lines which are 'more advantageous', in terms of giving a higher level of normed net output than actual wage costs plus normal profit. NNO really has to be operated on the basis of highly disaggregated coefficients, or else combined with highly detailed assortment plans. Either way, it is bad news for the people who actually have to work the details out.

But whatever the operational drawbacks of NNO, its development did represent some increase in the level of sophistication of Soviet planning. As we shall see in Chapter 5, a similar experimental trend in the investment and construction sphere extended to the disappearance of the traditional command principle as such. But on the general balance of centralisation the trend is at best equivocal, at worst in the 'wrong' direction, and this confirms the pattern we noted at the basic Material Balances level.

The essence of Brezhnev's economic policy orientation is perhaps most clearly evoked by the history of the Shchekino experiment in the 1970s. By 1980 altogether 2,003 enterprises and production associations were working on the full system, with a further 7,251 using 'specific elements of the method' (Fil'ev, 1983, p. 59). It is difficult to know precisely what this means in employment terms, but it is unlikely that as of 1980 much more than around 10 per cent of the Soviet industrial labour force was working under the full system. Reports on the effectiveness of Shchekino are uniformly positive. In the Shchekino combine itself (now renamed the Azot association) 1,814 men − 23 per cent of the work-force − were made redundant during 1967–80, with labour productivity increasing 4.1 times over the same period. In industry as a whole, 968,000 persons, representing 6 per cent of the total work-force, were made redundant during 1976–80, and the money saved in 1980 alone, in terms of wages fund economies, amounted to 287 million rubles (Fil'ev, 1983, pp. 58-9). The method is also credited with a sharp reduction in the rate of labour turnover (Mirgaleev, 1977, pp. 104-5). Why did the Brezhnev leadership not extend it further? There seem to be two main groups of reasons − technico-planning obstacles to universalisation, and fears that it might ultimately work *too* well.

The first problem the Soviet authorities encountered as they tried to push the system outside the chemicals industry was that the technology and history of many key sectors, e.g. engineering, simply do not suit Shchekino as originally developed. In straightforward production line industries with limited product ranges, like the energy sectors, chemicals and petro-chemicals, substantial scope was found for the conflation of jobs – nearly half the redundancies at Azot from 1967 to 1980 came into this category. But a Leningrad survey showed that the scope for that kind of economising of labour in engineering plants is quite limited (Fil'ev, 1983, p. 61). What keeps labour productivity down in machine-building is the prevalence of large, non-specialised factories, carrying full complements of auxiliary processes and services operating on an under-capitalised, labour-intensive basis. This of course, is a very specifically Soviet form of overmanning, induced by the powerful tendency to organisational autarky we discussed earlier. To break the pattern would require: (a) a solution to the basic supply problem; (b) a major restructuring of production profiles. These requirements take us far beyond the limits of the Shchekino method – indeed they take us right back to the general planning issues posed in 1965.

Secondly, superior bodies were often less than sympathetic to the experiment. Ministries failed to make appropriate adjustments to wages funds in connection with major investment programmes, leaving some enterprises without the funds to pay Shchekino supplements. Gosplan and the Ministry of Finance changed the rules so that any Shchekino economies in wages funds not used to pay supplements had to be transferred back to the state budget. Throughout the 1970s workers found themselves deprived of Shchekino wage supplements as new wage tariffs were drawn up (Fil'ev, 1983, pp. 67–8) – note how once again the ratchet rears its ugly head. Given the pressure on managers to retain some surplus labour for all the reasons we discussed earlier, and given the sometimes dubious and ephemeral nature of the material incentives, it is not clear that there was a consistently powerful motivation for managers or workers to follow the method.

Perhaps most important of all, the Brezhnev government baulked at the danger that large-scale redundancy might turn into large-scale unemployment. It is very significant that the Shchekino system was widely introduced only in highly dynamic sectors like chemicals, where it was possible to reabsorb most of the redundant labour within the same enterprise or association. Nearly half of the total number of workers made redundant in industry from 1976 to 1980 were found new jobs at their existing place of work (Fil'ev, 1983, p. 59). The development of labour placement services during the 1970s obviously strengthened the basis for reabsorption of redundant workers, but, as many Western countries have discovered in the last ten years, labour from traditional heavy industries can be extraordinarily difficult to redeploy. For the typical Soviet worker, with a low real wage and little effective participation in decision-taking, the kind of job security which only white-collar workers enjoy in the West has been a major focus for identification with the system. To the extent that Brezhnev's political base was as much among the traditional working class as among the Party apparatus, it is not difficult to see why he was reluctant to be over-hasty in the extension of the Shchekino system.

As we saw in Chapter 2, the post-reform wager on the foreign technology card did not work. Soviet growth rates fell steadily from the mid-1970s onwards, and nothing happened to modify the adverse productivity trends already strongly in evidence in the early 1970s. Part of the reason for this lies in the fact that neither the reform nor the reaction substantially touched two of the weakest areas of the Soviet economy – agriculture and investment/construction. We will be discussing the special problems of those sectors in the following two chapters. In addition, as energy material extraction costs in the Soviet Union rocketed, the rental element in Soviet oil and gas export revenues diminished, while commitments to supply energy to East Eupopean allies became economically increasingly onerous. In January 1975 a system was introduced whereby intra-CMEA international trade prices were calculated on the basis of a five-year moving average of world prices, adjusted annually (Economic Commission for Europe, 1977b, pp. 124–5). This ensured an improvement in the terms of trade for the Soviet Union, as energy prices were pulled up towards the world level, but it also meant that as long as the trend in world energy prices continued upwards intra-CMEA delivery prices could never quite catch up.

More generally, however, Brezhnev surely erred in believing that planning reform and increased import of technology could be anything but *complementary*. Western specialists disagree on the impact of technology transfer on Soviet economic performance (Gregory and Stuart, 1981, p. 403), but it is beyond dispute that its impact has been substantially below its potential, simply because of inefficiency at the assimilation stage. A study of a group of chemicals turnkey projects exported from the UK to the Soviet Union came up with an average total lead-time, 'from first enquiry to completion (handing over)' of

6 years and 10 months, as compared to a corresponding figure, for projects done in Western Europe, of 2.25–3.5 years. Thus the Russians are almost as slow at completing imported as domestic investment projects, *even where all the construction and installation work is done, or supervised, by Western firms.* Some of the 'excess' in the chemicals sample related to negotiating time, but even the contract completion stage took on average 2.5–3.0 years longer than it would in Western Europe (Hanson and Hill, 1979, p. 594).

Quite apart from this, and quite apart from the very specific problems with success-indicators, etc. which the moratorium on reform inevitably entailed, the 1970s witnessed the onset of a degree of sectoral rigidity which made effective policy initiatives increasingly difficult. It is ironic that the experiment with decentralised investment was wound up essentially in defence of the sacred priority principle, because that principle seemed increasingly ineffectual as the Brezhnev era progressed. We touched on what may be part of the reason for this in Chapter 2 — increased reliance on the ratchet principle to provide an approximation to plan consistency necessarily produced a tendency to structural conservatism. More fundamentally, however, the process of escalation of priorities which had begun on the death of Stalin had come to its logical conclusion. Thus the Economic Commission for Europe, in relation to Eastern Europe as a whole:

> one possible explanation for the slow pace of change in investment structures, apart from resistance to change within the existing structure, may lie in the multitude of criteria for investment priorities. Export promotion, orientation towards domestic resources and the consumer market, savings in labour, fuel and raw material inputs, increased intensiveness in research and advanced technology, are only the most frequently quoted. The application of so many priority criteria in the allocation of investment resources may slow down changes in the pattern of investment allocation, and produce mixed tendencies in relation to planned developments. (Economic Commission for Europe, 1978, p. 76)

The issue of economic reform, then, would not go away, and 1979 promised to be the worst year yet for growth rates. It came as no surprise when a new planning decree was published in July 1979.

The 1979 'Mini-reform'

The main features of the decree were as follows ('V TsK KPSS . . .', 1979; 'Obuluchshenii . . . ', 1979):

(1) Success-indicators: in sharp contrast to the optimism about the role of profit in 1965, the 1979 approach saw no surpassing virtue in any single indicator. Sales would continue to serve as the basis for assessment of fulfilment of contracts (with the implication that there would be no incentive for overfulfilment) ('Planovye pokazateli . . .', 1979). Profit would still figure as an indicator, but in some cases, presumably those of planned loss-making enterprises, would be replaced by cost-reduction. The precise role of NNO as an *output* indicator was left vague, but it was specified that NNO should, as a general rule, be used as the basis for calculating labour productivity, now established as a key success-indicator. Ministries would continue to have plans for gross output, as would some associations and enterprises. Increased stress on details of assortment (cf. earlier remarks about NNO), and increased optimism about the possibility of measuring quality directly, gained expression in the notion of 'output in natural terms' (*proizvodstvo produktsii v natural'nom vyrazhenii*) as a key operational indicator ('Planovye pokazateli . . .', 1979). Bonus funds would be formed out of profits with the fund-forming norms calculated on a profit base. These norms would relate to labour productivity, deliveries and assortment/quality (Hanson, 1983, pp. 5-6).

(2) Transition to the production association system was to be completed by 1981-2.

(3) Integrated and comprehensive incentive fund arrangements were to be introduced from 1981 at ministerial, industrial association and production association levels.

(4) The conservative interpretation of direct links was to be universalised by 1980.

(5) Stable norms (i.e. no ratchet principle) and symmetrical bonus systems (i.e. no Micawber principle) were to be (once again) introduced. Unused remainders of funds should be carried over to subsequent years.

(6) Ministries should stop chopping and changing plans. In particular, they should not normally adjust plans downwards. But they should have the power to allow associations and enterprises to reduce levels of production, and modify associated planning indicators, if this permitted introduction or increase in production of high technology

goods, or new high-quality consumption goods. They should in addition be permitted to establish a reserve of up to 5 per cent of total investment votes.

(7) Counter-plans, once adopted, would now count as part of the state plan for plan-fulfilment assessment purposes. Special bonuses were to be created for 'rate-busting'.

(8) Renewed emphasis was placed on the development of wholesale fairs.

(9) Decentralised investments financed from the production development fund should be decided on independently by the association or enterprise, but then incorporated into the ministerial plan. The number of sources of finance for decentralised investment was, however, programmed for reduction, and above-plan profit was specifically excluded from that number ('Poryadok . . . ', 1979).

(10) The brigade system of work-team organisation developed in construction (see discussion in Chapter 5) was to be extended economywide.

(11) The Shchekino system was programmed for generalisation, with special supplements of up to 50 per cent of basic wage payable from wages fund economies. Management was to be allowed greater freedom in disposing of these economies. Upper limits on enterprise work-forces were to be established.

(12) The number of commodity groups planned at the central level was to increase.

(13) Ministries were to prepare by 1980 'passports' for each association and enterprise, on which would be stated all basic technical information about the organisation, especially in relation to capital stock.

(14) There was to be a shift in emphasis away from short-term towards medium-term and long-term planning. The five-year plan should form the crux of the planning system, and twenty-year programmes for scientific and technical progress, broken down into five-year periods, should be worked out, and corrected every five years. Gosplan should in addition elaborate a ten-year outline of strategic lines of development on the same revolving five-year basis.

(15) Rental elements should be taken more into consideration by planners. A systematic water charge to enterprises was to be introduced.

This is a difficult piece of planning legislation to assess. There seems to have been a kind of paralysis in Soviet policy implementation in the last few years of the Brezhnev era; no doubt the increasing rigidity of the structure of the economy may have been partly responsible for this, but there was also a purely political element relating to the expectation of a change in leadership. In any case, that change came within a little more than three years, with the death of Brezhnev in October 1982. Rather than attempt a systematic follow-up on the provisions of the mini-reform, then, we may find it more useful to study those provisions simply as a basis for pin-pointing the preoccupations of the Soviet government of the time.

The first thing that strikes one about the 1979 decree is its internal inconsistency. The items listed under (6) seem to pull the long-suffering ministries half in the direction of greater tautness, half in the direction of more slackness. On the same basis (5) stands in flat contradiction to (7). Partial autonomisation seems to be back in vogue, with encouraging noises about wholesale fairs, and a slightly ambivalent statement about decentralised investment. At the same time the degree of centralisation of the basic plan construction process is to increase, while the new full array of success-indicators, if they are all to 'bite', must likewise represent an increase in the overall level of centralisation. More specifically, with profit pushed into the background and the position on NNO very non-committal, the success-indicator proposals to a great extent seem to boil down to a return, directly or indirectly, to gross output – what else can 'output in natural terms' mean in a Soviet-type economic system? And when we see formalisation of the reintroduction of cost reduction as a success-indicator – something which had been happening *de facto* since 1974 (Dyker, 1983a, p. 33) – we must wonder whether the Soviet leadership can actually remember as far back as 1959.

The trend towards greater centralisation highlights the inconsistency of the decree by making a nonsense of the stated aims of killing the ratchet principle and improving medium- and long-term planning. How can planners with even more work to do eschew use of their tried and trusted rules of thumb? How can Gosplan, which has always notoriously neglected the long term because the short term made such impositions, possibly switch resources and manpower to five- and ten-year perspectives?

The reform decree does, in fact, bear all the marks of a compromise between different pressure groups. There is still a nod in the direction of the once-ascendant marketisers, but it is the 'perfect computationists', among the professionals, who were clearly holding the stage in the late 1970s. They believed that they could raise the number of

Figure 3.1: The Organisational Structure of the Soviet Economy as Envisaged by the 1979 Planning Decree and Associated Measures

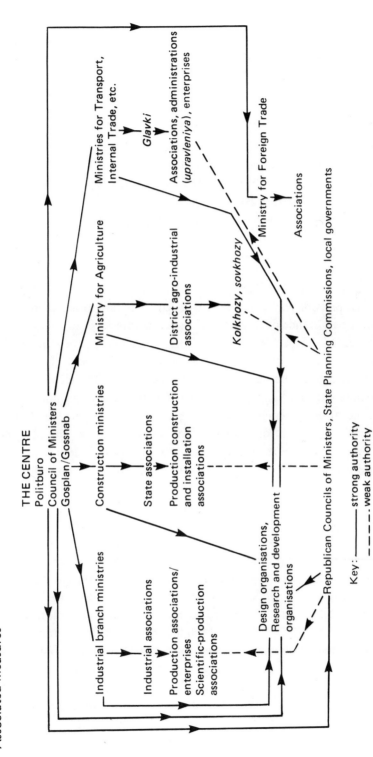

commodity groups centrally planned from *c.* 15,000, presumably on the basis of computerisation, though no Soviet Input-Output table has ever numbered more than a few hundred sectors. They must have believed that on the same basis the process of 'passportisation' of Soviet industrial capacity could eventually make it possible to assess production capacity directly, without use of the ratchet principle. Certainly there has been some success in using computerised input-planning systems, in which the stage of indent (*zayavka*), the stage where the water is usually poured in, is dispensed with (Rabinovich, 1976, pp. 209-10; Cave, 1980, pp. 108-9). But as Martin Cave's detailed research has shown, the development of computer networks in the Soviet Union has been hampered by general systemic problems as much as any other potential source of 'intensification'. So powerful, for example, is the imperative to organisational autarky that even mini-computers have been produced by handicraft methods in dwarf-workshops (Conyngham, 1982, p. 120). It is now more than ten years since the existence of a system of linked computers capable of inverting matrices of 15,000-20,000 was first reported in the United States (National Bureau of Economic Research, 1974, pp. 103-5). There is no evidence that the Russians yet dispose of such hardware systems.

Where the marketisers and perfect computationists may not be in substantial disagreement is on the questions of the balance of tautness/slackness. It was surely the hand of an *apparatchik* that sketched in the bits about 'rate-busting' and 'no downwards adjustments'. The whole logic of the traditional crude growth maximisation strategy does, of course, lie precisely in the notion that when growth rates falter trouble-shooters can be sent out to 'chivvy people up'. It is a logic familiar to bureaucratic structures around the world, a logic which an *apparatchik* stratum threatened with the fate of the dinosaur may be *politically* bound to pursue. It is, of course, a false logic.

As we suggested earlier, not a great deal happened between the publication of the 1979 decree and the death of Brezhnev. By the end of 1980 NNO was being used as an actual output indicator in only a small proportion of the total number of industrial enterprises and the situation may not have changed a great deal by 1982 (Hanson, 1983, p. 2; p. 12, n. 13). There was, as far as we can tell, no rapid extension of the Shchekino system, and indeed a follow-up decree on labour problems placed primary stress on labour discipline, looking forward to the Andropov era ('O dal'neishem . . .', 1980). The impetus to further rationalisation of the price system implicit in the decree was sustained through a comprehensive price reform carried out in 1981-2, which brought energy prices into line with secular production cost trends, without abandoning the principle of average-cost pricing (Hanson, 1983, p. 2). To the extent that use of value-added and profit as success-indicators demands a consistent price system, this was of some importance. But of course nothing had happened to make producing units more responsive to prices. We can only speculate as to whether planners were becoming more sensitive to shadow-prices. As the Brezhnev era drew to an end, it was difficult to avoid the impression that, at least in relation to economic planning, the Soviets, like the Bourbons, never forget anything and never learn anything.

From Andropov to Chernenko

Much more even than with the late Brezhnev era, we have to try to assess the economic initiatives of the men who succeeded Brezhnev in terms of *a priori* analysis, rather than investigation of results. There is an additional problem, inasmuch as the new era has seen the publication of very few decrees on the planning system as a whole. Rather we have to try to spot key policy articles, trusting that they in some sense represent the official view. This is a slightly risky business, but it does place policy formation in a rather livelier perspective than the language of decrees permits.

One of the earliest and sharpest delineations of the essential Soviet economic problem came in an article published in *Pravda* soon after Brezhnev's death (Kulagin, 1982). The author started by citing some basic statistics on the engineering industry which strikingly confirm general patterns that have formed much of the foregoing material. The average Soviet engineering enterprise employs 1,600 men – in West Germany the figure is less than 250. Productivity in Soviet plants is, however, much lower. A large part of the explanation for this stems from just that feature of Soviet machine-building that makes it unsuitable for the Shchekino system – a substantial proportion of the 'extra' personnel in the typical Soviet enterprise are low-productivity auxiliaries working in dwarf-workshops. In the Soviet engineering industry repair, instrument and transport/warehouse work account for 38 per cent of the total work-force, compared to just 11 per cent in the United States. In the West the size, in terms of work-force, of the average engineering plant has fallen quite sharply over the recent decades, with the development of 'micro-specialisation'. The Soviet Union has quite simply missed out on this micro-specialisation revolution.

The *Pravda* writer picks up an idea that had been put forward at a conference specially convened to discuss the problem in the early 1970s — the creation of a specialised Ministry of Inter-Sectoral Production (Ministerstvo mezhotraslevykh proizvodstv) which would centralise production of all 'bits and pieces'. He suggests that such a ministry could be allowed to build up its own network of optimal plants without any forcible closing-down of existing dwarf-workshop capacity — in time other ministries would happily close them down themselves and switch their orders to the cheaper and better lines produced by the new specialist ministry.

There are two obvious attractions about this proposal. First, it aims to solve the success-indicator problem which has always militated against production of 'fiddly little things' by creating a *powerful* organisation which by definition produces nothing else. Secondly, it implies a fairly radical marketisation of a crucial area of the Soviet economy, since it argues that the new ministry should prosper through the forces of competition. At the same time, it suffers from serious weaknesses. It is not clear where the initial human and capital resources for the new ministry might come from in an economy with already overstrained labour balance and investment front. More generally, it says nothing about the underlying problem of over-centralisation. One of the reasons, we are told, why the original proposal from the early 1970s did not get off the ground is that already overworked central planners simply did not have the time to go off designing new ministries. And if the Ministry of Inter-Sectoral Production were really to be established on a semi-market basis, surely the system would run into exactly the same problems as arose when they tried to autonomise decentralised investment and subsidiary industrial activity in the late 1960s and early 1970s. With the general supply problem still unsolved, main-activity engineering enterprises might well simply refuse to trust the new ministry, preferring to stick with their costly but sure in-house supplies. If the confidence barrier were indeed broken, and the new venture well and truly set up, how would supply links with the rest of the economy (after all, everyone needs nuts and bolts) be regulated? By command, by the market, by the pushers? More fundamentally, what degree of autonomy would the Ministry for Inter-Sectoral Production be given in relation to its own investment plans, etc., and how would all this fit in with the central investment priorities about which the authorities got so upset in 1971-2? Of course, the *Pravda* article was not a blue-print, only a discussion piece. But it raised a number of issues which would be taken up in more official materials the following year.

Rather more down to earth was Andropov's immediate clamp-down in the area of work discipline. As we saw, there had been a labour degree focusing very much on this problem in 1980, but it was left to Andropov to get tough on the kinds of easy-going shop-floor practices which had developed after the death of Stalin. No doubt the policeman's mentality introduces a personal political element here, but Andropov's discipline drive does surely also reflect a judgement that sheer shop-floor effort might be a key variable in any revolutionising of the Soviet labour productivity situation. A report from early 1983 (Tuganov, 1983) cites the case of a bricklayer who had refused to do work outside his strict professional field. His on-the-spot punishment was an effective wage-cut. Judgement would surely not have been so summary under Brezhnev, but one could cite dozens of similar examples from the Soviet press over the past year or so.

Not surprisingly, then, the post-Brezhnev regime has also shown itself fairly well disposed towards the idea of planned redundancy. Articles have been published praising the Shchekino system (Fil'ev, 1983; Aparin, 1983), and a report on a Shchekino-type system in operation in a Leningrad scientific-production association describes substantial redundancies without any redeployment within the association. In some cases engineers have been obliged to take shop-floor factory jobs (Semenov, 1983). Key policy articles and decrees have also once again stressed the importance of improving labour placement procedures (Oblomskaya *et al.*, 1983; 'V TsK KPSS . . . ' 1983, p. 4). Now of course none of this is new, but it does appear that Andropov, while recognising like Brezhnev that the Shchekino system can only be as good as the labour placement system, may have been prepared to countenance a higher level of unemployment in the Soviet Union than his predecessor. Nothing authoritative on these matters has appeared since Brezhnev's successor died, but here as elsewhere the Andropov line seems to be holding for the time being. The problem with this whole approach to the labour productivity problem is that it tends to move in abstraction from the general planning problem. Just as Shchekino gets stuck, *inter alia*, because with supply uncertainty only a fool gets rid of 'surplus' labour, so improved labour discipline may get stuck for precisely the same reason. But it would be unfair to suggest that the new leadership has not realised this. On the contrary, a decree of August 1983 explicitly recognised the link between the discipline problem on the one hand and the supply problem, indeed the total planning problem, on the other.

Ministries and departments and business leaders fail to create at some enterprises, building sites and farms the necessary organisational and economic conditions for normal, high-productivity work. Inadequacies in planning, material-technical supply and the organisation of production lead to lay-offs, storming, excessive overtime, and to non-fulfilment of plan targets and commitments. This in turn affects discipline and, in the last analysis, rates of growth of productivity. ('V TsK KPSS . . . ', 1983, p. 3)

Rather the difficulty appears to come in recognising the crucial link between supply problems, etc. and the underlying problem of over-centralisation. Yet Soviet academic economists seem to have been emphasising precisely that crucial link in their deliberations in early 1983.

In April 1983 Tatyana Zaslavskaya of the Siberian filial of the Academy of Sciences presented a paper to a closed seminar in Moscow which attacked the whole issue of the historical context of the Soviet planning system. The paper argued, in much the terms that we have argued in this book, that the centralised, command economy had a good deal to recommend it during the period of the 'Great Leap Forward', but cannot cope with the size and technological complexity of the contempory Soviet economy. In particular, it cannot solve the labour productivity problem. More specifically, planning difficulties were blamed on an overmighty and overweight intermediate planning establishment, which stands accused of obstructing and distorting communication between Gosplan and actual producing units. It appears that the paper was received with some displeasure at Politburo level, but a decree was published in July 1983 ('V Tsentral'nom Komitete KPSS . . . ', 1983) setting up an experimental system to be run in a number of heavy and light industrial ministries from 1 January 1984, which seems to aim, *inter alia*, to follow up this idea.

The main elements in the experimental system are as follows:

(1) As a general principle, the role of production associations and enterprises in the drafting of plans is to increase. At the same time, assessment of plan fulfilment is to become more rigorous. This implies a reduced role for ministries and industrial associations in plan drafting *and* in the process of 'adjustment' whereby traditionally intermediate planning bodies have guaranteed achievement of the aggregate plan, while ensuring that most subordinate organisations would report plan fulfilment. Plan implementation should become more parametric, with fewer commands and more 'norms'.

(2) Key success-indicators will be sales/deliveries for all producing units, and where appropriate 'development of science and technology', quality, growth of labour productivity, and cost reduction or increase in profit. Profit will continue to be the source of finance for the bonus fund, but will apparently lose its special role in relation to fund-forming norms.

(3) 'Stable norms' for wages funds, incentive funds, etc. are to be established on a five-year basis.

(4) No bonuses will be paid to managerial workers unless sales/ deliveries plans are met.

(5) Autonomous production association/enterprise control over decentralised investment, financed from the production development fund, is to be re-established. Production units will also enjoy greater freedom in financing 'technical re-equipment' (*tekhnicheskoe perevooruzhenie*) from amortisation allowances and credit.

(6) Production associations and enterprises are to be permitted to use moneys from the association-level Unified Fund for the Development of Science and Technology to finance autonomous R and D work, and to compensate for increased costs in the period of assimilation of new products.

(7) Producing units are to be allowed more independence in deciding the allocation of the socio-cultural and housing fund.

(8) Management is to be given greater independence in the use of bonus funds and wages-fund economies accruing through job rationalisation.

(9) Budgetary rules are to be changed so that production units can retain a larger proportion of profit on a regular basis. This implies that the various incentive funds are to grow in size as well as independence, though it may also imply an increase in the proportion of centralised investment financed from retentions. 'Payments into the state budget are to be made by production associations (enterprises) on an autonomous (decentralised) basis.'

A good deal of this is reminiscent of 1979. The success-indicator regime differs only in that there is no mention of NNO, 'stable norms' make another weary entrance, the resuscitation of the decentralised investment is more emphatically programmed, while the principle of allowing management the financial freedom needed to give the Shchekino system a chance is reiterated. The general emphasis on autonomy of disposal of enterprise funds, on the other hand, smacks of 1965 rather than 1979. But there are some genuinely new elements, in particular the idea of downgrading the role of the intermediate planning body, and bringing the producing unit into more direct contact with the central planners. As we noted in Chapter 2, the Soviet planning system has always been a little anomalous in that plan construction has been almost wholly concentrated in the central planning organs, while responsibility for overseeing the execution of plans has been largely devolved to the ministries. The approach in the experimental decree could cut out a lot of the inter-level overlap in Soviet planning, and in principle pave the way for a more consistent, multi-level system, as ministries and industrial associations concerned themselves with a limited number of commodity flows, leaving them more time and energy to concentrate on medium-term investment and R and D matters.

But the whole thing is married up with a success-indicator/incentive constellation which modifies the command principle but little, while in practice it seems to complicate rather than simplify centre-periphery relationships. Thus

> planned deductions into the material incentive fund are calculated on the basis of rates of reduction of costs. For every percentage point of cost reduction this year the planned base year size of the material incentive fund increases by 5 per cent. In addition, a stable norm for deductions from accounting profit is established. In case of non-fulfilment of the cost-reduction plan the planned level of profit will not be achieved, which will reduce the rate of deductions into incentive funds. (Goncharov, 1984)

What on earth is this supposed to add up to? And what happens when you bring quality, productivity and innovation, not to mention deliveries, into the picture? The planners seem to be simply making work for themselves. They may, furthermore, have deprived themselves of a crude, but powerful, weapon, namely the facility to leave most details of execution to a number of ministries — which in most cases could plan that execution in terms of fairly homogeneous physical output — small enough so that they, the central planners, did not need the ratchet for that particular set of planning relationships.

The re-statement of the stable norms goal confirms that, once again, the Soviet authorities are being optimistic about getting rid of the ratchet. This is odd, for two reasons. First, the reaffirmation of the straight modified Micawber principle in relation to sales/delivery plans suggests that crude growth maximisation tactics are still not a thing of the past; it must also, as we saw earlier, make the ratchet the more necessary in relation to informational problems. As if to underline this point, some enterprises in the experiment are reported to be re-introducing *unmodified* Micawber, with top bonuses for *over*fulfilment (Kulenis, 1984). Secondly, the elements of decentralisation in the experimental decree do not represent any fundamental shift in the planning balance. As we saw, the success-indicator/incentive arrange-ments seem to be fussier than ever, while on the supply side the exper-mental decree really does very little. Why, asks the Minister of Local Industry of the Lithuanian republic – one of the organisations involved in the experiment – should the Ministry not allow enterprises and associations to sell over-plan production on the basis of direct agree-ments, and without allocation certificates? (Simenenko, 1983). Why, in cases where enterprises are being conceded the right to fix temporary prices on new consumer goods, cannot they also be permitted to pro-cure the necessary materials without having to go through the whole Gosplan/Gossnab system? (Plyatsuk and Andrusenko, 1984). Most important of all, how can an enterprise with formal powers of dis-position over investment funds hope to concretise these unless it is permitted to negotiate flexibly with suppliers? As we saw from the experience of the 1965 reform, supply would probably have to be decentralised rather radically if that kind of enterprise autonomy were to be meaningful. The experimental industrial planning decree *in itself* does remarkably little in this direction. Since it is only an experiment, operating within the milieu of an industry still largely operating on the rules of the Brezhnev era, its effect on the general level of central-isation of the Soviet industrial supply system must be negligible.

The partial, experimental nature of the new decree has created other, more generally motivational problems. The Soviet press has been full of complaints about ministries dragging their feet (Valovoi and Nikitin, 1983), and enterprises failing to brief their workers properly. It is perhaps not surprising if the attitude of the average veteran man-ager is that 'when we get some kind of feedback from the experiment, then we'll talk about it. But what it's going to give us I don't know right now. We've only had suggestions, and there's nothing hard to go on' (Ovdienko, 1984). The current leadership seems committed to following the experiment through. Prime Minister Tikhonov has characterised it as ' . . . a broad, perhaps the broadest ever, search for and elaboration of the most effective principles and methods of planned socialist management of the economy' (Tikhonov, 1984). At the same time he reveals that the Party has decided to press forward with a 'Programme for the Complex Perfecting of the Management Mechanism'. That sounds as if it might upstage the industrial planning experiment, but the Prime Minister is at pains to stress that there is no need for ministers and managers to sit around waiting for the new programme. They have quite enough independence, he asserts, under the experimental system. He may not mean that, but if he does he is obviously wrong. The 1983 decree does nothing significant about the overriding problem of the planning system — over-centralisation. For that reason its positive initiatives on the autonomisation of enterprise finance, especially in relation to decentralised investment, are likely to come to naught, as the economy remains dominated by the ratchet principle and supply uncertainty. Thus the experimental decree reproduces the partial approach of the *Pravda* author from late 1982. Issues of selective autonomisation of the planning system are discussed with a degree of clarity: but they are never placed against the backdrop of *the* planning problem.

4 THE SPECIAL PROBLEM OF AGRICULTURE

General Assessment

Soviet agriculture performance over the last decade or so has been disastrous. With around 20 per cent of the work-force still employed in the sector this must obviously have had a serious direct effect on national income performance, quite apart from any dislocations that may have occurred when agricultural deliveries to industry have fallen below the planned level. There cannot be the slightest doubt that bad luck with the weather has had something to do with this — even in 1983 the sweltering spring which Russia enjoyed while Western Europe shivered was bad news in terms of germination (*Research on Soviet and East European Agriculture*, 1983), and in the light of this performance in that year was really not bad at all. Nor can there be the slightest doubt that in Soviet natural conditions North American yields are quite simply unattainable. But the extent of the failure of the agricultural policies of the Brezhnev government must incline us to suspect that organisational problems have been at least as important as acts of God in inducing the generally dismal production and productivity record displayed in Table 4.1.

Yet the new regime of 1964 seemed to start off by doing all the right things. During Khrushchev's last years price policies were less favourable to agriculture than they had been in the late 1950s, and this, combined with other policies, had conspired to halt the movement towards more investment and better incomes on the *kolkhozy*. Brezhnev and Kosygin re-established the earlier trend, and by 1975 collective farmer income from work on the *kolkhoz* alone was approaching 60 per cent of the average for non-farm workers, with *sovkhoz* incomes very nearly at the level of those of non-farm workers by that year (Schroeder and Severin, 1976, p. 629). Taking the private sector into account, the gap between farm and non-farm incomes in the Soviet Union is certainly now no greater than it is in many Western countries. Between 1966 and 1969 the great majority of *kolkhozy* were able to abandon the traditional labour-day basis for remuneration and substitute a standard minimum monthly wage (Dyker, 1976, p. 136). Investment inputs into collective agriculture have also risen steadily throughout the post-1965 period, and agricultural investment as a

Table 4.1: Rates of Growth of Soviet Agricultural Output and
Productivity, 1966–83

	Output	Output per Agricultural Worker
1966–70 average	4.0	6.7
1971	1.1	1.8
1972	−4.6	−4.2
1973	16.1	15.6
1974	−2.7	−3.1
1975	−6.3	−5.4
1976	6.5	6.5
1977	4.0	4.4
1978	2.7	3.1
1979	−3.1	−2.4
1980	−2.5	−2.0
1981	−1.0	−0.6
1982	4.0	3.6
1983	5.0	

Sources: Official Soviet and UN statistics.

proportion of total investment held at the extraordinarily high figure
of 20 per cent throughout the 1970s (Economic Commission for
Europe, 1977b, p. 100; 1983, p. 140).

We saw in the last chapter that the late 1960s and early 1970s were
a period of unusually flexible attitudes to subsidiary industrial activity
in the countryside, and this flexibility was mirrored in approaches to
the internal organisation of the farm. The tradition of arbitrary Communist Party interference in *kolkhoz* and *sovkhoz* affairs through the
medium of a special breed of trouble-shooter who might descend on
a particular farm at any time was laid to rest, for the time being at least,
with the declaration that 'the plenipotentiary has been abolished'
(Yagodin, 1968, p. 26). The number of products carrying a compulsory
procurement target for each farm was reduced, permitting farm managements to take a much more positive policy line on specialisation
(Gray, 1979, p. 546). But the reaction which caught up subsidiary
industrial production in the early 1970s could not fail to touch agriculture itself. The initiation of vast land improvement schemes like the
non-Black Earth Programme, inaugurated in 1974, inevitably meant
renewed interference in farm affairs, with blue-prints for new field
systems and crop rotations coming from specialist design organisations
rather than from the farms themselves (Kopteva, 1983). The development of various kinds of inter-*kolkhoz* and mixed *sovkhoz/kolkhoz*
associations facilitated the development of a new *dirigisme* in relation to

basic agricultural as well as subsidiary industrial activities. By the early 1980s production trends were calling into question the wisdom of this, as of every other aspect of Brezhnev's agricultural strategy. Decrees of November 1980 ('Ob uluchshenii . . .', 1980), 1982 ('V Tsentral'nom Komitete KPSS . . . ', 1982), the latter published simultaneously with the Food Programme for the period up to 1990, laid out a new planning structure for the sector which remains in force to the present time.

The 1982 decree singled out three major flaws in the existing system of agricultural planning and management. Firstly, it was top-heavy, overstaffed and fragmented. Secondly, and partly flowing from that, it had failed to marry up sectoral and territorial aspects of planning. Thirdly, there was too much administrative interference in the running of actual farms. The decree set out the following basic elements to a new approach:

(1) The independence and scope for initiative of farm managements should be increased. *Kolkhozy* and *sovkhozy* should be viewed as the key links in the system of socialist agriculture. Specifically a consolidation and expansion fund, distinct from the production development fund, was to be created for the finance of state farm decentralised investment on the basis of a 5 per cent rate of deduction from profits.

(2) With a view to improving the link-up between territorial and sectoral planning, and to slimming down administrative staffs, *district agro-industrial associations* (RAPOs) should be created. These would include not only farms, but also enterprises involved in agricultural supply, agricultural processing, etc. They would thus cut across lines of departmental subordination. They would not have independent staffs, but would use the apparatus of the district agricultural administration, a routine local government body. Agro-industrial associations would also be created at the provincial/autonomous republic level.

(3) By contrast with the situation in at least some of the older types of agricultural association, the constituent farms and enterprises of the RAPOs would, in conformity with (1) above, retain their *khozraschet* status. Nevertheless the RAPO would take over a number of operational planning roles, viz.:

(a) Break down aggregate control figures into specific procurements targets for state and collective farms: check draft plans of other organisations, and present any suggested modifications to the appropriate hierarchial superior.

(b) Distribute investment votes, budgetary grants and credits, and equipment and other supplies to farms; reallocate, subject to the agreement of the organisations concerned, 10–15 per cent of the material-technical supplies allocated to other enterprises, etc. attached to the association.

(c) Centralise, on the initiative of farm or enterprise managements, specific production and business functions; subcontract such functions to specialist organisations, irrespective of administrative subordination, or create subdivisions for their execution.

(d) Set prices for intra-association transactions, irrespective of administrative subordination.

(e) By agreement with the appropriate hierarchical superior, reallocate unused capital investments (it is left unclear whether this means funds or equipment) between state organisations within the association.

(f) Create centralised incentive funds on the pattern established by the 1965 planning decree, these presumably to operate in parallel with farm and enterprise incentive funds: sanction farm and enterprise rules for the distribution of bonuses to management.

(g) Work out medium-term development plans.

The provincial/autonomous republic agro-industrial associations were programmed for a much less operational role in relation to short-term planning. They would only 'examine' (*rassmatrivat'*) basic production indicators, while being empowered, with the agreement of republican ministries, to reallocate investment and material-technical resources. Like the RAPOs they would have the right to centralise specific but unspecified planning and management functions and subcontract them. Beyond that their main area of interest would be medium-term development plans.

(4) A network of agricultural scientific-production associations was to be developed. It should concern itself with the design of management systems and incentive schemes as well as strictly agronomic research.

(5) Following up the general principle enunciated in the 1979 planning decree, stable five-year fund-forming norms were specified as the basis of agricultural planning.

(6) The procurement price system was to be reviewed, with the introduction of improved prices for cattle, pigs, sheep, milk, grain, sugar-beet, potatoes and vegetables as from 1 January 1983.

(7) Financially weak collective farms would now be eligible for budgetary grants to finance infrastructural investment, and also to help

meet insurance claims. (Hitherto only state farms had enjoyed this privilege.)

(8) A total of 9.7 billion rubles' worth of debts owed by weak *kolkhozy* to Gosbank were to be written off, interest payments lifted and a ten-year moratorium declared on repayment of a further 11 billion rubles' worth.

(9) Farm directors would have the right to autonomise the activity of peasant work teams on the basis of a 'collective contract'.

Much of this is not very new. Soviet politicians and planners have been worrying about the coordination of sectoral and territorial planning at least since the time of Khrushchev, and one of the prime lessons of the Khrushchev period is surely that this problem is not solved by creating yet another planning body. But the general idea of concentrating specific pricing and investment planning powers at the association level, while consolidating the independence of the actual farm in relation to day-to-day production matters, seems sound enough. The systematic concession of any substantial rights of price formation to a body outside the centre is, indeed, somewhat revolutionary in Soviet terms. On the other hand, the partial autonomisation of farm investment funds will surely run into exactly the same problems that it has in the industrial sphere. More important still, is the increased emphasis on parametric planning being balanced by less reliance on direct physical planning? What exactly do the new arrangements mean in terms of the number of compulsory procurement targets per farm? The 1982 decree seeks to increase the stress on procurement plan fulfilment in connection with bonuses for procurement organisations ('V Tsentral'nom Komitete KPSS . . .', 1982, p. 18) and one subsequent report confirms that the number of procurement targets set by RAPOs for farms may in fact be increasing (Kopteva, 1983).

The massive writing-off of *kolkhoz* debt and the extension of budgetary grants to the collective sector has clearly been necessary to maintain 'normal' profitability on farms (see discussion of investment policy below), but it has exacerbated problems of short-term financial planning. The difficulty with credit amnesties, as the Yugoslavs have discovered (see Dyker, 1983b), is that they may create the expectation of further credit amnesties. Sure enough, we find a Gosbank official complaining recently that

Over the last few years a number of *kolkhozy* have been lax in relation to finance, and have failed to set aside enough, or in some cases any, funds from income for the replenishment of indivisible funds [i.e. fixed capital stock − D.A.D.]. They have diverted working capital to fixed capital formation, and simply not worried about paying back credits advanced by Gosbank. In a word, they have tried to carry on business at the expense of the state ... Some farm managers appear to suppose that state funds are given to them not for raising the effectiveness of production, but for covering financial deficits which arise not only because of unfavourable weather conditions, but often as a result of bad business practice and wastefulness. (Pilipas and Polozenko, 1983)

Thus Soviet planners are faced with an interesting dilemma in their attempts to refine agricultural planning. Because they want to make planning more parametric, they want farms to be more cost-conscious, and in particular they want them to count the cost of investment more carefully. Some of the factors militating against such a change in attitudes are purely historical-institutional − the fact that traditionally there have been no planning norms for the volumes of working capital required by collective farms, the fact that short-term Gosbank loans to *kolkhozy* carry a rate of interest of only 1 per cent: of course, as long as procurement targets had absolute priority, while the labour-day system ensured that the *kolkhoz* wage bill was a pure residual, such financial details could hardly have mattered. The political decision to pay collective farmers a decent regular wage coincided with the shift in Soviet priorities towards efficiency considerations, and with a political decision to sink large volumes of investment into agriculture. Meanwhile the system of compulsory procurement targets was retained, if modified. But how can the Soviet authorities isolate the results of 'bad business practice and wastefulness' in a situation where they themselves retain strict control over the basic production profile of farms, and retain substantial control over fixed investment in the sector? In the real world where X-efficiency problems may be paramount, and investment appraisal a most uncertain affair, the optimal combination of price and output planning may clearly be a very tricky business.

Finally, better prices and new bonus funds will obviously do no harm, but the crucial question in relation to incentives is how they get through to the ordinary peasant. That is why the new rights conceded to farm directors in relation to autonomous work-teams are so important. Here, indeed, we touch on an aspect of Soviet agricultural organisation that may be of far greater importance than changing details of bureaucratic hierarchies above the farm level. If, indeed, we peruse the history of the link (*zveno*) system over the past couple of decades, we will obtain a much more dramatic perspective on these wavering trends towards a more autonomous agriculture.

Intra-farm Centralisation and Decentralisation

The essence of the traditional collective or state farm was summed up in the institution of the *brigade*. Up to a hundred strong, performing general agricultural tasks under orders which might change from day to day, the brigade epitomises the extensive utilisation of unskilled labour, and the total alienation of the agricultural worker from the decision-making process. Thus the brigade has symbolic as well as organisational importance, and exactly the same can be said about the radical alternative to it, the link. The link is a small unit, often of less than ten people, which is allocated a particular piece of land to work, or a particular specialised function. The link was in favour with Stalin himself in the late 1940s, but fell sharply into disfavour in 1950. In the late 1950s and early 1960s Khrushchev ran a link campaign – without great success, perhaps because he placed emphasis on the 'crop-attached' link, which has to move from one piece of land to the next with the crop rotation (Pospielovsky, 1970, pp. 425–6). The autonomous, or 'normless' (*beznaryadnoe*) link, which came to the forefront in the late 1960s and early 1970s, is simply given a small piece of land, if it is lucky the necessary supplies and equipment, and left to get on with it. No specific set tasks are handed down, only an aggregate sales plan, and members share on the basis of stable norms in the profits of over-plan sales (Kolesnevov, 1971, p. 23). The emphasis in the early Brezhnev period on the 'land-attached' link represented a clear recognition of the tremendous psychological importance of giving, or rather returning, some real sense of 'mastery' of the land to the peasants (Kopysov, 1968, p. 10).

Yet in 1971 I. Khudenko, architect of the highly successful Achki integrated link system, one of the most advanced decentralised forms, was imprisoned on trumped-up charges. He later died in jail (Katsenelinboigen, 1978, p. 66). This by no means spelt the end of the link, but it did represent a reassertion of the power of the Communist Party apparatus men – in this case the rural Party secretaries – exactly paralleling the elements of economic policy reaction we discussed in the last chapter. Rural *apparatchiki* clearly felt that autonomisation was going to far, and they were also worried about the fact that many autonomous links were being operated by family groups (Ivanov, 1968).

Just as the oil price hike strengthened the hand of the conservatives in relation to planning as a whole, so the bumper harvest of 1973, following on a couple of poor years, gave confidence to rural reaction, and seemed to indicate that the clamp-down on autonomous links and subsidiary industrial production was paying dividends. The result was that the 'normless' idea became distorted out of all recognition in the mid-1970s, with norms, indeed, re-encroaching with a vengeance on the activity of agricultural work-teams. Emphasis shifted towards the 'autonomous' brigade. In principle, under this system the brigade council administers, and can modify, the pattern of incentive payments to members, with direct farm-peasant relationships being reduced to a minimum (Bakhtaryshev, 1980). Under full brigade *khozraschet*, the primary production unit is supposed to operate as a quasi-independent mini-enterprise, with sales, wages fund and material costs the only planned indicators coming down from farm level (Revenok and Pichugin, 1981). The autonomous link, of course, does not even normally have wages fund and cost plans, and the size of the brigade must in any case mean less effective autonomy for the individual peasant than under the link system. But the trend back to more bureaucracy and more interference tended to neutralise the autonomous content of link and brigade systems alike. Even where the link pattern survived, it tended to become over-bureaucratised and over-complex (Aksenov, 1980). Farm incentive schemes in general became so complex and confused that actual payments had in many cases to be made on a basis of 'common sense' — no prizes for guessing whose common sense!

More seriously, the ratchet principle reasserted itself emphatically in centre-farm and farm-work-team relationships, with peasants' wages in some cases actually falling as productivity rose (Aliev, 1980). If we glance back at Table 4.1 it is not difficult to see why this happened. The hopes raised high in 1973 were dashed in the succeeding years, and, as we reasoned in the last chapter, the instinctive *apparatchik* reaction to a growth crisis is to go back to crude growth-maximising tactics. But with the re-establishment of the incentive to hold back production levels, so that succeeding years' plan targets would not be too demanding, the basic rationale of the autonomous work-team — that members should in some sense be profit-sharers — was destroyed. As we noted earlier, the decrees of November 1980 and June 1982 on agricultural planning asserted the principle that targets should be set on the basis of average actual production levels over a five-year period. This seems as over-optimistic as any other stable norms slogan, but reports from the early 1980s spoke of farms on a specialised brigade system working with three-year norms, coupled with special rules to stop earnings shooting ahead of productivity (Bogomolov, 1982).

However sceptical we may be about self-denying ordinances in relation to the ratchet, there can be no doubt that there was a change in attitudes towards autonomous work-teams as early as 1980. The most striking development has been the so-called 'hectarer' (*gektarshchik*) system, introduced in tobacco- and tea-growing, viticulture and potato farming in Azerbaidzhan, Transcaucasia. The hectarer system goes beyond the autonomous link idea by organising work on the basis of *individual* land attachment. Manuring, irrigation, application of pesticides, etc. is done on a brigade or farm basis. Hectarers are allotted a hectare and left to organise tending of crops on a personal basis, perhaps with some help from the family, but with no interference from above – though crop pattern is, of course, still centrally determined. *There appear to be no formal norms at all. Gektarshchiki* are simply paid a uniform price per kilogram, however much they turn in, and annual earnings of as much as 3,500 rubles – at least double the average agricultural wage – are reported (Agaev, 1981).

Clearly we are verging here on the supersession, in all but name, of the *kolkhoz/sovkhoz* system as such. But the sub-tropical areas of Transcaucasia may have enjoyed special arrangements in the past as well, and there has been no sign of any extension of the hectarer system to the less exotic agricultural areas of the Soviet Union. It has its opponents as well as supporters even at home, and the Azerbaidzhan Agricultural Research Institute has branded it as excessively individualistic and a hindrance to mechanisation. But just as the reappearance of the ratchet in agricultural planning in the mid-1970s came as no surprise, so we can perceive the recurrence of a pattern in the new relaxation of the early 1980s. Under Stalin, under Khrushchev, and in the early Brezhnev/Kosygin days, Soviet agricultural policy has often exhibited a surprising degree of pragmatism in the face of deep and prolonged crises, and this has formed a marked counterpoint to the frenetic tradition of the plenipotentiary, which, as we have seen, has dominated in relation to short-term problem-solving. It is not surprising, then, considering the continuation of weak growth trends into the 1980s, that intra-farm autonomisation has remained as firmly on the new leadership's agenda as it was on Brezhnev's in his last year.

In 1981 as many of 18,000 formally autonomous links were operating in the Russian republic (Dudorov, 1982). Brezhnev underlined the provisions of the 1982 agricultural planning decree with a call for more personal initiative and responsibility and less 'petty tutelage' in his speech on the Food Programme for the period up to 1990 (Brezhnev, 1982, p. 5), and more genuinely normless interpretations of the link system soon started to appear in the Soviet press again. Under the rubric of the idea of collective contract (see discussion of the 1982 decree above), links were to be formed voluntarily, with an elected link leader (*zven'evoi*), and all forms of bonus distributed on a democratic basis. The farm should make cash advances to the link, and undertake not to reallocate equipment and operatives (*mekhanizatory*) without the agreement of the link (Petrov, 1982). 'The operatives', we are told, 'remember each other's birthdays, and help each other with their private plots. What need I say about their work in the fields?' (Kozlov, 1982). Even if we take all this with a large pinch of salt it clearly represents a sharp contrast with the situation in the late 1970s. Yet the same sources pin-point at least one major reason why the whole thing may again come to naught. Links have been disbanded because in poor harvest years, which have been the rule rather than the exception, link members, with higher absolute output performance, were receiving lower payments than ordinary piece-workers (Petrov, 1982). Once again, the extraordinary hardiness of the ratchet principle is underlined.

The post-Brezhnev leadership has committed itself to following through the policies of the Food Programme and the 1982 agricultural planning decree on intra-farm autonomisation ('Rezervy agrarnoi ekonomoki', 1984), and there have been wide-ranging reports of the development of the collective contract idea over the last year or so. The basic principles of that idea, as reiterated in new legislation, are as follows:

(1) Links are formed voluntarily.
(2) Personnel cannot be arbitrarily reassigned.
(3) Relations with the farm are on the basis of free contracting, but planned tasks for output and quality are binding, once contracted.
(4) Fund-forming norms are on a stable, five-year basis. Contract prices are either constant or sliding, with higher outputs attracting higher prices.
(5) Distribution of wages and bonuses is decided independently by the link. (Mukhtarov, 1983; 'Kollektivnyi podryad . . .', 1983)

In practice the pattern seems to be extremely varied. One report speaks of a transformation in work-team-farm relationships, a renewed personalisation of the link with the land, with the fields being called after the individuals who tend them, and a determined educational drive to unteach farm administrators their 'bad habits' of administrative interference in link affairs (Konovalova, 1983). Others, by contrast, portray a situation where operational independence seems to be focused on Andropov's favourite god-child, labour discipline, and principles of remuneration are kept firmly under the control of the farm management. We can illustrate this point by looking at two key features of the typical collective contract.

First, labour evaluation cards (*karty otsenki truda*) for each work-team member are made out by the peasants themselves, taking into consideration quality of work, good time-keeping, etc. Secondly, there is the labour coefficient (*koeffitsient trudovogo uchastiya* – KTU). There seems to be some variation in the way that KTUs work, but the basic principle is that the KTU should determine the basic wage and the bonuses of a work-team member, and that it should in turn reflect, wholly or partly, the content of the labour evaluation cards. The key point is that the value of the KTUs themselves is determined by the farm, not the link or brigade. Thus, while the peasants are left to do the *monitoring* of each individual's work input, it is ultimately the farm which decides what the value of that input should be (Primakov, 1983; Emchenko, 1983). A cynical observer might see in this no more than an enlistment of the peasants themselves in the campaign for better work discipline, a downwards extension of the dubious privilege of 'keeping an eye on your workmates'. But in other cases even the labour evaluation cards are made out by the management (Vasil'ev, 1983a). It is difficult to see what meaning the collective contract can have under those conditions.

We can, however, find cases where the collective contract idea has been interpreted in a much more genuinely normless way. In one cattle-breeding *sovkhoz*, for example, 'the *sovkhoz* pays . . . 4.64 rubles per centner of weight gain and 1.25 rubles per head for above-average fatness of animals at point of sale. The collective itself [i.e. the work-team – D.A.D.] decides how the resultant payment is divided up' (Sadykov, 1983). Similar arrangements are reported to have been hugely successful in Kazakhstan market gardens (Ulubaev, 1983). A random sample of articles provides no basis for assessing the incidence of different interpretations of the collective contract, either over Soviet agriculture as a whole or in particular subsectors. But it does appear that farms are to a considerable extent being left to make their own arrangements, in accordance with the principles of the Food Programme, and that most farms are plumping for a fairly cautious variant.

Does that mean that we can write off the collective contract as a serious policy alternative? I think not. The principle of collective incentive payments is surely a sound one, whoever sets the norms. The fact that the family-based link is now once again respectable (Ulubaev, 1983) must provide a great fillip to motivational levels. What the experience of the 1970s showed, however, was the extent to which *any* attempt to create more flexibility at the work-team level in agriculture could be neutralised by the inherent tendencies of the Soviet planning system as a whole. It is hardly surprising that we read reports of the voluntary principle in the formation of links being violated (Platoshkin and Utkin, 1983). The whole essence of traditional Soviet approaches to planning lies in the right of management to reassign men and materials as priorities change and bottlenecks develop. Certainly all the economic arguments suggest the increasing value of a more balanced approach as the economy matures. But is it reasonable to expect farm managements and rural *apparatchiki* to change their approach if their superiors continue to insist on a wide range of compulsory but often erratic procurement quotas? Thus, while links may be more important than RAPOs, they may in the last analysis depend heavily on the quality of the RAPO environment if they are to function properly.

One obscure, and possibly sensitive, issue relating to the link is that of employment. The traditional brigade had, as we noted, a certain rationale in the context of the persistence of a substantial degree of overmanning on farms. The fact that the scope for large-scale transferral of labour from country to town became progressively restricted in the post-Stalin period does not mean that *kolkhoz* and *sovkhoz* work-forces had been slimmed right down to a minimum. Rather it reflects the fact that a large proportion of the remaining rural population was elderly, often female, with little education and formal skills. They could not easily be used in any other occupation but low-technology farming. With 20 per cent of the total work-force still in agriculture there must at the present time still be a great deal of scope for rationalisation of farm work patterns, and it is not surprising that the reports just cited speak of 50 per cent reductions in the manning of links in connection with the introduction of the collective contract.

What is at first sight a little surprising is the claim that the autonomous link system improves activity rates (Konovalova, 1983). This does make sense, however, at the strictly work-team level in connection with the high degree of job interchangeability which is such a marked feature of the contemporary approach to the link system. As we saw in the last chapter, Andropov was very keen on job interchangeability, and indeed saw it as an aspect of discipline as well as of organisation. There is, of course, no reason why the elderly and/or unskilled should find themselves excluded from many types of link. The fact that the big mechanised jobs are still done by the farm, even under the hectarer system, the tendency for links to be family-based, must imply substantial flexibility in terms of the structure of labour supply to the work-team. But if the links are economising on labour, and if output levels remain on a given dimension, simple arithmetic tells us that at the level of the farm as a whole there must be some danger of redundancy. This may help to place in perspective the renewed emphasis, through the RAPOs, on subsidiary industrial production. It may also reveal a hope that a revolutionising of output levels will, *à la* Preobrazhenskii, guarantee full employment with much reduced labour-output ratios (Volkov, 1983; Nasyrov, 1983).

Finally, a technical planning point which has arisen in the course of the airing of the collective contract issue ties in nicely with some of the points from Chapters 2 and 3. It is quite common under contemporary link arrangements for the 'plan' to be simply the existing level of production, often on a five-year average basis. This obviously represents, among other things, a recognition of the fact that aggregate agriculture output is quite simply not growing systematically at the present time. It does strictly, then, mean an end to the ratchet principle. It does not, however, change the principle of *planning from the achieved level* one whit. Rather it merely applies that principle with a zero mark-up. One might be tempted to see therein the abandonment of the crude growth maximisation aspect of this aspect of planning tactics. In fact, the zero mark-up idea has been endorsed precisely as a way of stopping 'soft' farm managements fixing negative mark-ups, thus making it possible for peasants to receive bonuses when production has actually dropped (Volkov, 1983).

The Private Sector

No one can dispute the general importance of the private sector in Soviet agriculture. In 1979 that sector still produced as much as 26.5

per cent of total Soviet agricultural output (Shmelev, 1981, p. 69). It remains crucially important most obviously in relation to supplies of fresh fruit and vegetables. What, the reader may ask, has the private sector got to do with planning? The answer is: under contemporary conditions a great deal. Where it has become the focus of the attention of the Soviet planners, at central and farm level, is in relation to the vexed question of fodder production. There was a substantial relative expansion of Soviet animal production in the period 1971-5, with an annual rate of growth of 3.3 per cent, as compared to one of 1.6 per cent for crop production. This expansion of livestock was wholly intentional, as the Soviet population sought to increase its consumption of meat products, in conformity with generally accepted notions about the relative income elasticities of different agricultural commodities, and in response to heavily subsidised meat prices. But the poor performance of the crop sector throughout the last decade has left the planning authorities with an embarrassing problem of how to feed the additional animals. That is why the Soviet Union imported some 11 per cent of its total coarse grain requirements throughout the period 1976-80 (Economic Commission for Europe, 1982, p. 207) and nearly 15 million tons of maize in 1981 alone (FAO, 1982).

To try to ease this most strained element in the Soviet agricultural balance, farm managements have been negotiating ingenious new deals with their peasants in their private capacity. Basically these involve farming out livestock – pigs and cattle – to the peasants to fatten on their private plots. In return for guaranteed supplies of fodder at reduced prices the peasants deliver a proportion of the resultant fatstock to the farm. A problem in the past has been that the peasants have not been allowed to sell their 'share' directly to the farm, but have had to take it to the local agricultural procurement centre. As well as inhibiting the development of cooperation this has let in speculators who go around farms offering high prices (Gomanov, 1981) – another good example of how bureaucracy and red tape breed pushers and spivs. But in Georgia a system has been in operation since 1977 whereby cooperating peasants can sell their private produce directly to the farm, though in this case peasants do undertake formal plans for sales to the farm (Veselov, 1979). In Abasha, in Georgia, collective farmers are allowed to keep 10 per cent of the *kolkhoz* maize harvest on plan fulfilment, and 70 per cent of over-plan production. In addition, the collective farms are (strictly illegally) giving *kolkhozniki* an extra hectare of land for private cultivation of maize – on the basis that they keep 70 per cent and give the farm 30 per cent of the output, and also agree to sell to the state 200 kg of meat per annum (*Radio Svoboda*, 1982, p. 2). Positive reports on this kind of arrangement, as with the more radical link-type systems, usually seem to come from the south. In the northern non-Black Earth region problems with fodder supply have been especially recalcitrant, and the younger generation have shown themselves unwilling to get involved in time-consuming – if idyllic – operations like hay-making. As a result the number of livestock in the private sector in these regions has fallen sharply in recent years (Sokolov, 1982). But there is clearly a desire to try to do something about this.

Where the authorities have been more prepared in recent years simply to give private activity its head is in agriculture outside the state and collective farms. Town dwellers are now being encouraged to work small plots of 0.05–0.1 of a hectare, and permitted to sell their surplus production without any interference whatsoever – ten years ago people would have been branded as parasites and speculators (Rumer, 1981). Even coal-miners are being encouraged to keep pigs (Monogarov, 1980; Telegin, 1983). But this kind of subsidiary agricultural activity is by no means limited to the private sector. Industrial enterprises are increasingly developing their own 'allotment' subsector, especially where waste heat, etc. can be utilised. The Ministry for Light Industry has, indeed, been issuing formal target plans for such production (Rumer, 1981, p. 568). Going beyond the vegetable garden level, the Krasnoyarsk aluminium factory has more than 800 hectares of pasture, grazing a herd of cattle which should soon reach a thousand head. The plan is to increase the pasture holdings to 3,000 hectares by 1990 (Trokhin, 1983). Development in the past has often been hampered by sudden changes in direction – from poultry farming to pig-breeding, from pigs to milk, and this once again confirms the instability of policies on autonomous agricultural activity. But the last Brezhnev years did see a substantial improvement in continuity, and the late General Secretary called for 'obligatory and systematic aid' from the state and collective sectors to the private in his speech on the Food Programme (Brezhnev, 1982, p. 5). The Programme also singled out subsidiary agriculture in industrial enterprises as a growth point (*Prodovol'stvennaya Programma . . .*, 1982, p. 5).

Almost immediately on taking power, Andropov pledged that the provisions of the Food Programme for the private sector would be followed through (Andropov, 1982, p. 2), and the present leadership seems set to continue this policy line (Dudorov and Kozlov, 1984). Recent reports confirm a persistent ingenuity in seeking ways of easing the meat and fodder balances. The director of the Scientific-Research Institute for Agriculture in the Far North has suggested that the hunting of Siberian partridge should be given over to organised links (he used the word *zveno*) of amateur hunters (Solomakha, 1983). The (rural) co-operative retail network in the Russian republic has been increasingly selling pigs for fattening to private individuals — more than 4,000 per annum in one district of Archangel province alone (Pavlov, 1983).

Autonomisation, Resource Flows and Agricultural Performance

Yet for all this renewed flexibility in relation to farm organisational forms, Soviet agricultural performance remains unimpressive. Given the unsettled character of government policy over a long period of time, this is perhaps not altogether surprising. The peasants have seen it all before, and lack of clear long-term prospects must induce quick profit-taking in the private sector and a degree of indifference in the socialist sector. To date, the post-Brezhnev leadership's initiatives in this area have been neither decisive nor radical enough to promise any fundamental transformation of attitudes even if the current policy orientation lasts much longer than have similar orientations in the past. We can conclude from the experience of the last ten or fifteen years that substantially improved remuneration may make little headway with motivational problems as long as the work-force remains basically alienated from the organisational forms imposed upon it. More controversial is the whole question of production inputs into agriculture. Can we really believe that such a colossal sustained investment effort has been a complete waste of resources? Or is it simply that land improvement schemes take a decade or so to show their return? The fact is that projects like the non-Black Earth programme have already had a decade to show their return. Certainly the rather crude investment appraisal techniques commonly used by Soviet project planners (see Chapter 5) may be peculiarly inappropriate for schemes involving outlays and putative returns over extended periods. Certainly the traditional failings of Soviet design organisations (again, see Chapter 5) may have been particularly damaging in an area where local knowledge and a light touch may be of the essence. The following report from a *sovkhoz* in Archangel province underlines this point.

It was in 1978 that the Archangel filial of Sevzapgiprozem [specialist agricultural design organisation — D.A.D.] introduced a field system and crop rotation on the *sovkhoz*. The trouble was that it was not properly grounded — economically or agronomically. And not because it couldn't have been so grounded. The fact is that the design workers left their science, so to speak, in their offices at the agricultural and planning organs, and brought with them a structure of sown areas put together without taking any account of actual conditions, or of the opinions of our own farm specialists. (Kopteva, 1983)

The effective writing off of 20 billion rubles' worth of *kolkhoz* debt in 1982, however proper an application of the sound economic principle that bygones should always be bygones, must represent an admission that the Archangel case has been anything but unusual.

To make matters much worse, resources spent on dubious grand schemes have not been spent on improving supplies of more everyday items to agriculture. A few years ago, a frustrated agricultural engineer wrote to *Pravda*:

My working day starts at six in the morning. I check on the work of the mechanisers in the tractor brigades and get the orders for spare parts. Immediately I go off to the *raisel'khoztekhnika* [district agricultural machinery centre], where I spend the whole day 'winkling out' the necessary components . . . For what, I ask myself, did I do five years in an institute of higher education? To become an 'expediter'? Well you don't need higher education for that. (Shirobokov, 1980)

Supply to links and private plots has been particularly unsatisfactory. Small mowing machines suitable for cutting hay on wooded and uneven land are not available to the private sector. Mini-tractors have been promised, but have not materialised (Sokolov, 1982). Similar problems have affected the work of the hectarers (Agaev, 1981). But the shortage of decent tomato-picking combines, which means that a large proportion of the Soviet tomato crop is wasted every year, illustrates how similar problems can affect the big, semi-industrialised operations as well (Vasil'ev, 1983b).

Thus figures on aggregate investment give a basically misleading picture of resource inputs into Soviet agriculture. Here is one area where the traditional tactic of using capital investment to create mobilisatory impetus, to forge 'creative' imbalances, would probably never have worked, even in a period when it was working quite well in industry.

It was certainly a signal failure in the 1970s and early 1980s. Perhaps the most insidious effect of all this has been to drive supply-hungry farmers into the hands of the pushers and speculators, as we saw happening with subsidiary industrial production in the early 1970s. Thus conservative policies breed more conservative policies as apparatus reaction springs to punish legal irregularities rather than do something fundamental about supply problems.

In creating the RAPO system, the Soviet planners have clearly had the supply problem very much in mind. The fortification of the new associations with vague rights of disposition over the organisations providing industrial supplies and services to agriculture was backed up by more concrete changes in the success-indicator regimes of those organisations. Sel'khoztekhnika, which supplies equipment, Sel'khozkhimiya, which looks after chemical inputs, and drainage and irrigation organisations should now be rewarded on the basis of the output and profit performance of the farms they serve ('V Tsentral'nom Komitete KPSS . . .', 1982, p. 18). We have reports of RAPO councils applying sanctions against erring Sel'khozkhimiya organisations (Dudorov, 1983), and of Sel'khoztekhnika coming in and building up covered service and storage areas (*mashinnyi dvor*) at the farm level (Sidorenko, 1983). But reports of recurrence of familiar old problems are more frequent.

In this connection the work of the Sel'khozkhimiya association which serves the farms of the district within the framework of the RAPO is in very poor order. Unloading of wagons goes on in the open air, often when it is raining, in places where various other things are lying about. More than once it has happened that nitro-ammophos has been rained on and spoiled before it could be picked up, or delivered mixed up with dolomite powder and broken the spreading apparatus. In a word, it simply will not do for us or our partners in the RAPO to treat fertiliser so carelessly and negligently . . . Lorries and combine harvesters are frequently out of service because of the acute shortage of particular components. Indents for cultivators, equipment for working the surface of the soil and mowers are anything but satisfied. It would appear that these headaches do not particularly worry our RAPO partner, Sel'khoztekhnika. (Filippov, 1983)

Or again, take for instance industrial enterprises. They often send us tractors and agricultural machines which have something wrong with them. The Tashsel'mash factory recently sent us four OGKh-28 sprinklers — the pumps don't work. A T-4 tractor arrived at the Uzbekistan collective farm from the Altai tractor factory — it has an irreparably damaged crankshaft. We have sent two telegrams to this enterprise requesting a replacement, but have still not had a positive reply.

Sometimes the republican Sel'khozkhimiya has to send us nitrate fertilisers instead of phosphate, or vice versa — because of supply breakdowns. (Iskinderov, 1983)

That last remark points to one of the reasons why the RAPO system has not revolutionised the supply situation to agriculture — the organisations involved can only supply as well as they themselves are supplied. The director of a Sel'khoztekhnika association remarks:

We've got used to being criticised. Of course, there are inadequate workers in any collective. But all the same many deficiencies are not our fault. For a start, stocks of spare parts are virtually non-existent . . . If we give GAZ-51 motors to the Bezhetskii repair factory — they haven't got any spare parts either. Anyway their work is poor, and we have no way of influencing them.

I have to say something also about the quality of machines that we get. Some combines, for example, you simply cannot assemble — the slots do not fit. (Dudorov, 1983)

Other planning problems with the RAPO system include the eternal one of prices — now much more important because of the policy of trying to make the planning system more parametric. Farms complain of extortionate prices for some services. While sheer miscalculation is no doubt an important element here, overspecialisation in repair centres, often leading to very high transport costs, has also been a factor (Dudorov, 1983; Sidorenko, 1983). Bureaucratic red tape means that Sel'khoztekhnika is delighted, in principle, to sign comprehensive installation and maintenance contracts, but will not actually supply directly to farms so much as an electric light bulb (Dudorov, 1983). A telling detail emerges from one report of unsatisfactory work by an irrigation organisation. Here the RAPO council took a special decision whereby the irrigation workers were integrated into the farm links and brigades, receiving cash advances per hectare in the same way as regular link and brigade members (Logach, 1983). It is not clear that with the given basic organisational structure of the Soviet economy this kind of idea can be pushed to its logical conclusion – after all, the irrigation workers must ultimately remain subject to the authority of the Ministry for Irrigation and Drainage. But it does confirm our earlier point that if links are to work properly they need a sympathetic RAPO environment. In practice, the RAPO appears to remain a fairly weak reed. As of mid-1983 'the work of the [RAPO] council had not attracted a great deal of attention, nor had it had any notable influence on the different aspects of the life of the district' (Filippov, 1983). Future General Secretary Gorbachev's assessment of progress by the spring of 1984 was not markedly more positive than that ('Rezervy agrarnoi ekonomiki', 1984, p. 4).

Current Agricultural Options

We have already seen that the new Soviet leadership has continued the cautiously pragmatic policies of the late Brezhnev period on the link and the private plot, etc. Up to now there has been nothing official to indicate anything but continuity with the rather heavy-handed approach of the 1982 decree on the relationship of agriculture as a whole to the rest of the economy. At the same time, authoritative discussion articles in the Soviet academic press suggest that there may be some more far-reaching proposals floating around. The focus of Soviet deliberations on radical alternatives for farm/non-farm relationships is usually the Hungarian system. Now Brezhnev publicly praised Hungarian agriculture on a number of occasions, without ever letting his admiration affect Kremlin decrees very much. It is very possible that the pattern under the new leadership will be the same. Nevertheless a 1983 article from a scholarly journal (Otsason, 1983) presents a particularly clear assessment of what are perceived by Soviet eyes to be the virtues of Hungarian agriculture. We can, perhaps, speculate a little on this basis how current thinking on the matter may be oriented.

   Otsason lists with approval the following key characteristics of the Hungarian agricultural planning system:

(1) A sceptical attitude to the virtues of large scale.
(2) Emphasis on the *quality* of industrial supplies to agriculture.
(3) No obligatory output or procurement plans.
(4) A complex system of (state-controlled) procurement prices, taxes and 'enterprise' funds, which aims to provide incentives while maintaining tight state control over general trends, including trends in wages.

(5) Inter-farm cooperation organised on a strictly voluntary basis.

(6) Wide scope for the development of subsidiary, including private subsidiary, activity in the countryside, with the emphasis on integration of these subsectors with the socialist sector.

Points (5) and (6) could have been taken out of the 1982 Food Programme, and all the elements under (4) are also present in the 1982 planning decree. It is item (3) which really stands out as un-Soviet. Whereas the 1982 planning decree seeks to combine parametric and physical planning, the Hungarian system, for agriculture as for industry, places almost exclusive emphasis on parametric planning. Item (2) contains nothing that the Soviet leadership would not be absolutely delighted with. On item (1) we have little to go on as far as farm size is concerned, though the collective contract idea certainly does make for smaller work-teams. What may, of course, inhibit Soviet imitation of Hungarian agriculture planning approaches is the sharp contrast in the situations of the agricultural sectors of the two countries. Hungary is a substantial net exporter of food; much of her exports are high-quality, low-bulk products, and physical output targets would be of little obvious relevance to a government which has, perforce, to concern itself above all with how to repay a foreign debt of $8 billion. The Soviet Union, on the other hand, is a superpower committed to maintaining a maximum degree of self-sufficiency in food, but with an agriculture that has only ever been able to produce systematic export surpluses at the cost of starving the peasants.

The leader of the Warsaw Pact did, in fact, report an agricultural deficit on balance of payments of around 7 billion rubles in 1982, and a very substantial proportion of that deficit was accounted for by coarse grain imports for animal feed (Food and Agriculture Organization, 1983; Smith, 1985). Thus crude output of basic crops is still a very important consideration for the Soviet authorities, and it would take a brave man or a foreigner to advise the Soviet government that the best way to get good output performance was to stop planning for it. Again, it is relatively easy for the Hungarians to talk of stress on quality of industrial inputs into agriculture. With free contracting a universal feature of Hungary's market socialist system, farms unhappy with the quality performance of a particular supplier can simply take their custom elsewhere. Thus if the present leadership were prepared to bite the bullet of abandoning the traditional Soviet system of procurement targets, it would immediately come up against the problem of how such a radically autonomised sector could fit in with the rest of the economy, which would, presumably, continue to operate in the traditional way. Would they, in fact, be prepared to abandon command planning for the whole agro-industrial complex, including service organisations like Sel'khoztekhnika and the procurement agencies? If so, what would happen to the light industrial sectors, including textiles, which largely depend on agriculture for supplies of raw materials? Would output/sales targets be abandoned for them too? As with some of the ideas which have emerged in relation to industrial planning, the agricultural speculations of the present regime seem to stop short of assessing the full implications of isolated elements of autonomisation in what remains a centrally planned, command economy. We shall return to this theme in the last chapter.

5 THE SPECIAL PROBLEM OF CONSTRUCTION AND INVESTMENT

In Chapter 1 we pin-pointed fixed investment as a key instrument of mobilisation in the early period of Soviet economic development, and specified the characteristic problems of excessive lead-times and capital cost escalation as flowing essentially from the strategy – 'wrong-headed' in neo-classical terms – of ample utilisation of capital. It is time now to put more institutional and operational flesh on this sketch, and to go on to study how the Soviet planning authorities have tried to change gear in the investment sector. We start by identifying the major actors in the investment process.

The Central Planners and Ministries, etc.

The key document of overall centralised investment planning, the title list, is perhaps a surprisingly brief document, normally about six pages, covering the basic technical, locational and cost character-istics of a given project. The 1979 decree sought, for the first time, to give title lists some kind of binding force, for suppliers as well as construction organisations (Boldyrev, 1979). This underlines the extent to which investment plans have lacked the true command element characteristic of short-term output plans. In the past, as we shall see in detail below, there has been very little in the way of parametric elements to fill this gap. But it is, nevertheless, the title list which gives an authority the legal right to proceed with a project. Investment undertakings worth more than 3 million rubles are characterised as *above-limit*, which means that the title list has to be specifically ap-proved at the centre. For *below-limit* investment, block votes go to ministries (for the bulk of production investment) and republican authorities (for the bulk of amenities investment), and it is those intermediate bodies which approve the corresponding individual title lists. As we saw, the planning decree of 1979 aimed to increase the specificity of the title list by laying down that it should henceforth include breakdowns of volumes of construction work by year. The tradi-tional weakness of the Soviet planning system in relation to lead-times is underlined by the curious anomaly whereby the centre has issued

Table 5.1: Normed and Planned Lead-times from Inception to
Full-scale Production, by Ministry (in years)

Ministry	Average Normed Lead-time	Average Planned Lead-time
Construction and Road-Laying Machine Building	1.9	10.7
Machine Building for Light Industry and the Food Industry	1.8	8.2
Chemical Machine Building	2.3	9.6
Heavy Machine Building	3.1	11.7
Electro-Technical Industry	2.0	7.6
Instrument-Making	2.4	8.0
Machine-Tool Industry	2.5	7.1
Vehicle Industry	3.1	8.4
Heavy-Industrial Construction	1.9	5.0
Industrial Construction	2.0	4.9
Building Materials	2.4	5.2
Milk and Dairy Industry	1.8	3.9
Food Industry	2.1	4.4
Coal Industry	4.8	9.6
Petro-Chemicals Industry	4.3	7.3
Power Industry	5.8	9.0
Light Industry	2.7	4.2

Source: Bronshtein, 1970, p. 40.

norms for gestation periods, while it is the ministries and republican governments which have specified *plans* for the same, even in the case of above-limit projects. Table 5.1 demonstrates the extraordinary divergences to which this has led. Thus when we talk of Soviet investment *planning* we are clearly talking about something which is really, by Soviet standards, rather nebulous. Just how nebulous is a question we will be returning to later on. We should, of course, always bear in mind the elements of decentralised, i.e. strictly non-planned, investment, which as we have seen, have been of substantial importance at certain times in Soviet economic history.

Only in the case of the 'most important' projects (formerly defined as those worth more than 150 million rubles) are the actual detailed designs confirmed by the central authorities. Even ministries and republican governments delegate much of the checking of designs to lower-level bodies. Specific issues like lead-times apart, then, how do the Soviet authorities, central and intermediate, go about ensuring that the design organisations which do the detailed drafting abide by some kind of basic efficiency rules in their choice of technology, etc.? Although notions of rate of interest, rate of return, etc. were formally outlawed during the Stalin period, Soviet engineers fairly quickly developed a simple, but serviceable, formula for assessing the relative merits of technologies with differing capital intensities in given production lines.

What they did was to compare the difference in capital costs to the difference (in the opposite direction) in running costs with a view to ascertaining how many years it would take the variant with lower running costs to pay off its higher capital costs. The approach is therefore a kind of marginal pay-off period approach, which can be stated formally thus:

$$t = \frac{K_1 - K_2}{C_2 - C_1}$$

where K is capital expenditure, C is running costs, including depreciation, and subscripts denote projects with identical output characteristics to be compared. The subscript $_1$ is used for the more capital-intensive, and the subscript $_2$ for the less capital-intensive. The more capital-intensive variant is considered preferable if t is less than a normative T. It is common Soviet practice to formulate the criterion in terms of *coefficient of relative effectiveness* (CRE), defined as

$$e = \frac{C_2 - C_1}{K_1 - K_2} \; ,$$

the more capital-intensive variant being considered preferable if e is greater than a normative E. A more general formulation, permitting comparison of more than two projects, is

$$C + EK = \text{minimum.}$$

Thus the coefficient of relative effectiveness can be made to serve the purpose of a general investment criterion, as long as we are concerned with strictly efficient considerations — how to do a given thing at least cost — rather than welfare considerations. In the *Standard Methodology for Determining the Economic Effectiveness of Capital Investment and New Technology in the National Economy of the USSR*, published in 1960, and the first official formulation of the CRE, it was the sole basic criterion presented, as it was in the revised 1969 version of the *Standard Methodology* (*Tipovaya Metodika . . .*, 1960, 1969). Those two editions did make some vague reference to a concept of *absolute effectiveness*, but it was only in the most recent, 1981, edition that the coefficient of absolute effectiveness was clearly specified as the increment in national income, value added or NNO against investment ($\Delta Y/\Delta K$, or if you like, the incremental output-capital ratio) for the economy as a whole, branches thereof or re-publics; and in terms of increment in profit or cost reduction against investment for associations, enterprises, etc.

The 1981 *Methodology* lays down norms for levels of absolute effectiveness which are to operate as 'gateways' through which blocks of investment projects should have to pass. The principle on which this norm is set for the whole economy for each five-year period is 'not lower than the average actual ratio for the previous five-year period'. In practice, for the period 1981-5, the reported aggregate relationship for 1976-80 – 0.14 – has been applied more or less unmodified. Sectoral norms for the same period vary widely – 0.16 for industry, 0.07 for agriculture, 0.05 for transport and communications, 0.22 for construction and 0.25 for internal trade, material-technical supply, etc. Because it is couched in terms of average returns on tranches of investment expenditure, rather than returns on specific increments to the capital stock, this indicator cannot operate as a general criterion for individual investment projects. Rather it simply provides a check on whether the economy as a whole, a specific sector or association, etc. is holding to the policy aims of the authorities in relation to the overall capital-output ratio. It does not by itself provide a guide to action in cases where a divergence from those aims is indeed diagnosed.

In assessing the role of formal investment appraisal formulae in the Soviet Union, then, it seems reasonable to concentrate on the CRE. There are three main groups of problems with the criterion. Let us start with its technical specificities. First, it ignores the possibility of capital expenditures occurring in more than one time period. Secondly, it ignores the possibility of variation in running costs over time. Thirdly, it includes depreciation in running costs. In fact, this last peculiarity works out as an advantage in the case of projects which do have once-and-for-all capital outlays and constant operating costs, and brings the CRE more or less into correspondence with the standard Present Value test (Dyker, 1983a, p. 105).

Where capital expenditures occur over a number of years, and/or where operating costs vary, the CRE may clearly be a rather inaccurate guide to efficient investment decision-making. Given the special diffi-culties involved in precisely specifying all the parameters of an invest-ment project, however, we should perhaps be a little cautious in criticis-ing a criterion which has the great merit of simplicity. The *Methodo-logies* do, in any case, give a formulation which can, in principle, be used to take account of these two complications, and which again almost reduces to the Present Value criterion (Dyker, 1983a, pp. 106–7).

Rather more serious, from the point of view of divergence from conventional approaches, is the fact that E has tended, at least until very recently, to be set at sub-clearing levels. The 1981 *Methodology* predicates a norm for the whole economy during the period 1981–5 of 0.12, as against estimates of the marginal product of capital (assuming lead-times as 'normed', etc.) varying from 0.15 to 0.25 (Vaag, 1965; Trapeznikov, 1970; Kantorovich and Vainshtein, 1967 and 1970). The range of variation in E by sector has in the past been as great as 0.1–0.33, and the 1981 *Methodology* narrows this only slightly to 0.08–0.25. Predictably, it is heavy industry which has benefited from low Es, with a figure as low as 0.06 reported for power in the late 1950s (Dyker, 1983a, pp. 107–8). Thus the Soviet planners have shown systematic preference to their favourite sectors in the structure of E by sector. In addition, by keeping the average level of E below clearing, they have ensured that rationing, i.e. essentially bureaucratic arbitrariness, would always be a necessary element in shaping the investment front.

In any case, the status of the CRE as an element in a command planning system has, like that of the title list, been ambiguous. The 1960 *Standard Methodology* was not made obligatory for design organisations (Bergson, 1964, p. 252), and one of the authors of the 1969 version noted at the time that

> much work remains to be done before these principles can be transformed into working instructions for each sector, ministry, department and their subordinate institutions. It is necessary to finish this work quickly, so that instructions for the different sectors can be properly confirmed this year. (Mitrofanov, 1969)

No confirmation that this work was carried through satisfactorily has come to hand. The 1981 *Methodology* has not even been vouchsafed the epithet *Standard*, and its preface emphasises its provisional status. There are special criteria methodologically similar to the CRE covering the import of equipment. All our qualifications about the planning role of the CRE apply to these also (Dyker, 1983a, Appendix).

Thus while parametric elements have been of some importance in the elaboration of investment plans, they have not been predominant. In order to understand fully the origin of the investment patterns peculiar to the Soviet Union we must, then, study the organisational pattern of the investment scene in some detail, in order to put some flesh on to the notion of 'bureaucratic arbitrariness'. We begin by looking at the design sector.

Design Organisations

There are around 1,800 of these in the Soviet Union, employing about 800,000 people. They are strictly backroom organisations, with no powers of approval or rejection of projects, and are normally subordinate to Gosstroi, the State Construction Committee, or to individual ministries. They do play a systematic, if subsidiary, role in general investment planning. Since 1971 they have been involved in the elaboration of sectoral and territorial 'development and location schemes' and may, in the case of large and important projects, be involved in the preliminary stage of 'examination of the technico-economic advisability of the envisaged project' (TEO). Once a client has a clear idea of what he wants, he presents the design organisation with an 'assignment for design work', and this forms the basis for initial requests by clients for funds (Dyker, 1983a, pp. 51-2). The first stage proper in the compilation of the 'design and financial documentation' of a project was, up to 1969, the 'design assignment', which included 'basic technical decisions aimed at securing the most efficient utilisation of labour, material and financial resources, in the operation of the envisaged project and in its actual construction' (Podshivalenko, 1965, p. 135). By a decree of that year the name was changed to 'technical design'. A further decree of 1981 again changes the terminology, this time to the unbelievably clumsy 'design with aggregated estimate cost of construction'. These word games are not of enormous importance, except in possibly confusing the student, but they do reflect a desire to make the design a more cost-conscious document (of this more below), and also a more integrated document. In the extreme case of total integration of the design proper and working drawings stages, the term 'working design' is used. We will from here on refer to the basic design documentation, which forms the core of the work of these organisations, simply as 'designs'.

Traditionally, the principal success-indicator used in this sector of investment planning has been 'volume of design work' – a variant of the standard gross-output success-indicator, usually measured in value terms. In the 1959–65 period cost reduction figured as a major indicator in design work, as it did in industry. The 1965 planning reform made little impact on design. Profit was introduced as a success-indicator without much difficulty, but the problem of finding an alternative measure of output, parallel to the introduction of the sales indicator for industry and elsewhere, has proved intractable. Under the old regime tranches of volume of design work had been calculated as a simple percentage of the total work to be done, and organisations often received payment for work that was in a quite unusable state. The new idea was to base planning on 'completed stages of design work'. In practice, the degree of arbitrariness in the definition of completed stages is often such that the improvement on the old system is marginal, and a contemporary author characterises volume of design work as still effectively the basic indicator for design organisations (Kudashov, 1983, p. 9). As we saw just now, the increasing concern with costs characteristic of the late Brezhnev era has percolated through to the design sector. The finance of design work, traditionally done through advances, was supposed to go fully over on to a credit basis by 1980, and the 1979 planning decree predicated that this should in the majority of cases be for completed designs, rather than stages (note that this affects financial flows, but not necessarily success-indicators and bonus entitlements as such). That decree also announced the general transition of design organisations on to *khozraschet*, to be completed by 1980. That this was to be a fairly limited form of *khozraschet* was underlined by the fact that design organisations still do not pay the capital charge. Design organisations are supposed to share to the extent of 5 per cent in the special on-time completion/quality bonuses introduced for the construction industry in 1979 (see below). The effect of all these attempts to get away from the crude volume of design work approach is in any case limited by the continued prevalence of piece-work as a method of payment of lower-level design workers (Dyker, 1983a, pp. 53-4, 57-8).

The Construction Industry

The organisational structure of the Soviet building sector is complex in the extreme. Traditionally organised in a hierarchy of ministries, *glavki* and trusts, the sector is divided up administratively on the basis of a rather odd mixture of sectoral, functional and territorial specialisation. There are three main 'bricks-and-mortar' ministries. The Ministry for Heavy Industrial Construction (Mintyazhstroi) basically covers the coal and metallurgy industries, but for historico-locational reasons does in fact do most of the basic construction work in the Ukraine and South-West Siberia. The Ministry of Industrial Construction (Minprom-stroi) has a similar duality of specification, involving, on the one hand, chemicals, oil-processing and petro-chemicals; and, on the other, the oil-rich regions of the Volga-Urals. The Ministry of Construction (Minstroi) concentrates on engineering, light industry, the food industry, etc., and also has its 'own' territories. The subordinate organisations of these ministries are all territorially specialised. But the installation of high-technology equipment, especially imported, is the preserve of the Ministry for Installation and Special Construction (Minmontazhspetsstroi). This is (in theory) a crack organisation, highly centralised, possessing a nation-wide network of *technologically* specialised *glavki* and trusts (Dyker, 1983a, pp. 72, 204-5) with a degree of regional specialisation only at the lowest level.

A decree of 1979 laid down that the construction industry should transfer on to the association system, with the clumsily christened *production construction and installation association* as the basic unit, replacing the trust. This measure has not, however, been fully carried through. By 1982, 180 PCIAs were doing just 10 per cent of total contractual construction work (Podshivalenko, 1983, pp. 91, 93). The most recent investment decree reaffirms the trust as the basic operational unit ('Uluchshat' planirovanie, . . .', 1984). Around 90 per cent of construction work is carried out by regular 'contractual basis' organisations, which may be subordinate to specialist construction intermediate organs or to clients. The rest is done on an 'in-house' basis by organisations, often small and *ad hoc*, invariably subordinate to client organisations.

As with the design organisations, the traditional principle success-indicator in the building industry has been a variant of gross output. 'Gross volume of work' is defined as the total value of work done, including unfinished work, plus the value of bought-in materials. During the period 1959-65 cost reduction had the status of major success-indicator in construction, as in other industries. As with design, the 1965 planning reform brought the immediate introduction of profit as a success-indicator, and the beginning of a series of attempts to find an alternative measure of work completed. Pilot schemes in the late 1960s experimented with various kinds of value-added-based indicators, but in 1970 it was total marketed output (*ob"em realizuemoi produktsii*) that was nominated as the official successor to gross volume of work, though the alternative indicators survived at the purely experimental level. Two problems quickly became evident with this modified sales indicator. First, it is, like straight sales, still a gross indicator. Secondly, it can run into the problem of arbitrarily defined stages in the same way as design indicators can. In the middle-late 1970s more than three-quarters of total construction work was being planned on the basis of conventional stages, usually defined in terms of type of construction work, rather than integral stage of project as such.

But the reform in construction did try to create a direct incentive for timely completion by establishing operationalisation (*vvod v deistvie*) as a third key success-indicator. This change was backed up by an attempt in 1966 to strengthen the procedures of the State Operationalisation Commission, so that it would only pass as completed new capacities capable of actually starting production. In the experimental Belorussian system, first set up in the mid-1970s in a couple of that republic's construction ministries, operationalisation becomes the key indicator. Significantly, that experiment also seeks to measure output purely on a completed project basis.

In construction, as in design and industry proper, changes in success-indicators were to be accompanied by changes aimed at increasing sensitivity to financial parameters. Not only would operationalisation of new capacity became crucial to bonus payments, it would also become the basis of payment for work done. By 1978, 60 per cent of total accounts for construction were being settled on the basis of completed project. (Under the Belorussian system, all accounts are settled on this basis.) But serious problems arose in connection with the finance of work in progress. It was clear that the new planning arrangements could not work properly on the basis of the old system of advances from clients, since advances are in practice indistinguishable from intermediate payments. On the other hand, exclusive use of the completed project indicator as a basis for settling accounts demands some method of computing putative output and profit by the quarter, if only so that bonuses can be calculated and credit flows regulated. This may help to explain why in 1979 85 per cent of total unfinished construction was still being financed from clients' advances.

Managerial innovation during the 1970s was not restricted to reform of success-indicators. There was also a trend to the extension of the *khozraschet* principle upwards and downwards from the level of the trust. The Belorussian Ministry of Industrial Construction was itself put on *khozraschet*, using the same indicators as its subordinate organisations, while the *khozraschet* brigade, commonly called the Zlobin brigade after the man who originated it, was widely introduced.

Similar to the link arrangement in agriculture, the Zlobin brigade system gives the work-team a specific task, extending over three months or more, the requisite supplies, etc., and leaves it to get on with the job, subject to an upper limit on total wages and bonus payments. The system is reported to improve the quality of work, shorten lead-times by up to 20 per cent, and raise productivity 20–25 per cent. But its success has been limited by supply problems — building workers are of course dependent on the outside world in a much more continuous way than agricultural field workers — and by the resistance of managers who find it too complex, and who are reluctant to give up their traditional prerogative to switch work-teams around, as priorities and the supply situation evolve. These problems may help to explain why the system has been introduced more successfully in residential than in industrial construction. It is, of course, much easier to break down the former than the latter into convenient 'building-blocks'.

None of this, then, was terribly satisfactory, and it is not surprising that the 1979 planning decree took another bite at the problem of how to plan construction. The basic principle was to be universalisation of the Belorussian system, which had shown clear, if modest, results in reducing lead-times and volumes of unfinished construction. This boiled down to the following main elements:

(1) Full transition to accounts by finished project or stage by 1981.
(2) 'Self-financing' to become a key financial principle.
(3) Further extension of the Zlobin system.
(4) Key success-indicators to be operationalisation, marketable output (*tovarnaya produktsiya*), profit and labour productivity, measured in terms of NNO or similar indicator.

Apropos of (2), is quite clear that self-financing means what it says in relation to working capital. Unfinished construction is to be financed from own resources or from bank credit. It is not clear whether it extends into the sphere of fixed capital, on the model of the Ministry of Instrument-Making. In relation to (4), experience with the Belorussian experiment showed that clashes could occur between the demands of the operationalisation and marketable output indicators, inasmuch as the latter implies saleability but not necessarily sale, thus once again representing only a very marginal modification of the gross volume of work indicator. A 1980 ruling stipulated that output could only be counted as marketable once the capacities involved were actually in operation (Podshivalenko and Evstigneev, 1980, p. 49). This would effectively turn the marketable output indicator into an alternative (quantitative) expression of the operationalisation indicator. But a contemporary source indicates that the problem remains unsolved, with marketable output being counted on the basis of State Operationalisation Commission certificates as issued, *before actual confirmation*. This can mean a divergence of up to one year's work between reported marketable output and operationalisation (Podshivalenko, 1983, p. 91).

A Gosstroi decree of early 1980 defined the concept of *normed conventional-net output* (*normativnaya uslovno-chistaya produktsiya*) as basically the normed wage bill, plus the sectoral average rate of planned accumulation taken as a percentage of the normed wage bill − clearly an alternative to NNO which can be used with planned loss-making enterprises. (As many as 25 per cent of construction organisations are loss-makers − Podshivalenko, 1983, p. 92.) It is this variant which has been largely used in attempts to refine the measurement of labour productivity in construction, though without great success. The trouble with normed conventional-net output is that because it ultimately depends in both parts on the normed wages fund, it creates an incentive to overbid for normed wages fund, in order to make it easy to execute a given volume of marketable output with less than normed wage expenditure, thus recording higher normed than actual net output. As we saw, NNO creates an incentive to execute a given volume of work with less than normed labour inputs, but the fact that the other element in the formula − normed profit − is completely independent serves as a constraint on overbidding for normed wage fund. For with given prices a higher normed wage bill should, *ceteris paribus*, mean a lower normed level of profit, leaving NNO coefficients unchanged, but incentive funds, production development funds, etc. reduced in size. Even if normed levels of profit are not adjusted, the value of any 'fat' on the normed wages fund will only get through to the NNO coefficients on a reduced basis. The absence of safeguards against overbidding of this kind with the normed conventional-net output indicator means that it can produce substantially exaggerated reported figures for labour productivity growth. In addition, it has been pointed out that normed conventional-net output does not actually introduce a positive incentive to economy on materials, though it obviates the incentive under the traditional system to use materials amply. Thus on general productivity grounds the experimental indicator obtains rather low marks (Kudashov, 1983, pp. 8-11).

It is not at all clear that there has been any systematic implementation of these 1979 measures. Contemporary sources still speak of the 'cult of the gross' as a central problem in construction. Success-indicators apart, the basic system of remuneration in the building industry remains heavily output-orientated, with about 85 per cent of workers on piece-rate systems of one kind or another. A special decree of 1979 did establish specific bonus coefficients relating to on-time completion and quality, but incentive-fund arrangements remain generally heavily output-orientated (Dyker, 1983a, pp. 81-3). The investment decree of 1984 returns to the fray, but without coming up with any substantial, clear-cut proposals for the organisation of construction (Uluchshat' planirovanie . . .', 1984).

'The More Costly, the Better'

There is, then, a very special paradox attached to the development of planning instruments in the design and construction sectors. Because of the unique character of many investment projects it is in practice very difficult to value design and construction work except in terms of the *actual* costs involved. Thus crude output maximisation can easily turn into crude cost maximisation. But because of the scale and lead-times of projects it is equally difficult to evolve any kind of operational sales-type indicator parallel to that introduced in industry. Thus the area of the Soviet economy which most badly needs to get altogether away from the cult of the gross is the one still most at its mercy. While one can place the crudity of early Soviet industrial planning into historical perspective, and see a certain hesitant logic in the course of planning reform since 1965, we must now really raise the question of *whether Soviet investment is, or ever has been, planned in any way whatsoever*. If we put this together with the points made about ministerial overbidding for investment resources in Chapter 1, we can build up a fairly comprehensive picture of the kinds of perennial problems that have affected the Soviet investment scene.

Let us start by going back to *raspylenie sredstv* — excessive investment spread. However substantial the element of pure overbidding, design and construction organisations have undoubtedly made an independent contribution to this problem. Delays in the delivery of technical documentation have presented chronic difficulties. Hold-ups in deliveries affected 1,293 projects, with a total estimated value of 58 billion rubles (nearly half the value of annual investment) in 1979. It is quite common for projects scheduled for operationalisation during the given plan year to be without working drawings, and design organisations have been blamed for 20 per cent of cases of failure to meet planned completion dates. The tradition of centralisation in Soviet planning has left a powerful imprint on the design sector, leaving it at once the victim and the instrument of 'petty tutelage'. As of the late 1960s only 20-35 per cent of the working time of design organisations was taken up by work on the actual designs, though the figure does seem to have improved to 40-60 per cent by the mid-late 1970s. The rest of the time goes on the process of getting approval for designs from various organs. Now of course the existence of the success-indicator problem does make some degree of scrutiny over design organisations imperative – the command principle always tends to beget centralisation. But top-heavy 'multi-level' checking by other subordinate organisations, each with their own axe to grind, cannot be expected to yield high returns to the extra time invested, and must be a substantial factor in excessive design work-loads.

Perhaps even more overwhelming has been the tradition of an extraordinary degree of detail in the designs themselves. Of course, under the given planning system, building organisations cannot be trusted to sort out the more economic details of designs, but most of them are now well enough equipped with engineers to permit some devolution of purely technical decision-taking; yet the design for the Lipetsk metallurgical factory, for example, filled 91 volumes and 70,000 pages, and that of the Baranovichi automatic production line factory 220 volumes. Sheer clumsiness in the way forms have to be filled in compounds both kinds of petty tutelage. In addition, design organisations are obliged to drop work on a given project when its planned time runs out, and go on to the next project. If we put all this bureaucratic clumsiness together with the success-indicator-induced incentive to maximise the volume of design documentation, we are a long way towards understanding the causes of chronic lateness in the delivery of documentation.

Yet there are other factors, less specifically internal to the design organisations themselves. The structure of the design sector is excessively complex, and it is the rule, rather than the exception, for design work on big projects to be shared among a large number of organisations, commonly as many as 50-70. Despite the multitude of different organisations, rational specialisation has often been lacking.

For instance, there are no large-scale specialised organisations serving construction in internal trade and catering. From the point of view of scale and specialisation, then, it has been difficult for design organisations to fulfil their 'production' potential. Would it not be rather easy for the Soviet authorities to effect a substantial improvement here? In practice, no, because so many design organisations are departmental, and atomisation in design is to a considerable extent a function of the powerful tendencies to organisational autarky which we pin-pointed in Chapter 1 as a major obstacle to the intensification of the Soviet economy. 'Dwarf design organisations, duplicating the work of existing units, continue to sprout in our town . . . It would appear that this happens because of some deep-seated tendency to departmentalisation. So the organisation's small, well at least it's mine!' (Kirillov, 1975.)

Backwardness in design techniques has been a further factor slowing down work tempi. This has no doubt partly been conditioned by quantitative success-indicators, but has been exacerbated by the politically conditioned reluctance of the Soviet government to permit wide distribution of photocopying equipment. Lastly, design organisations do a great deal of work on projects that have not been finally approved – between 1962 and 1966 design work on above-limit projects valued at 12 billion rubles was left unused (the annual value of total investment at that time was around 50 billion rubles). This is clearly related to ministerial overbidding for investment resources – 'for many clients the design has become simply a document on the basis of which resources for construction can be obtained' (Kudryadtsev *et al.*, 1968, p. 51). As well as further increasing the burden of work on the design sector, that kind of bureaucratic politics must also breed considerable contempt for the whole investment planning process, delivery dates included, amongst design workers content to plod on and earn their bonuses for *val* (Dyker, 1983a, pp. 59-63).

We saw in Chapter 1 that delays in the investment cycle make it difficult to keep capital costs under a close rein. Table 5.2 illustrates the extent of the problem of cost-hikes on big projects. The average degree of escalation has been 30–40 per cent over the last couple of decades (Dyker, 1983a, p. 63; Kuz'mich, 1983, p. 55). Note that these figures cover only cost-hikes that are eventually absorbed into the official estimates, and some escalations occurring at the construction site level may never be so absorbed. The notoriously inflationary trend of Soviet machinery prices, particularly with regard to special pieces of equipment not covered in the standard price lists, has certainly been a factor in cost-hikes, both directly and as a basis on which design

Table 5.2: Cost Escalations on Selected Projects (million rubles)

	Estimated Costs	
	Envisaged for 1973 in the Five-Year Plan	Confirmed by the Annual Plan for 1973
Ust'-Ilim hydro-electric station	690.3	1,025.0
Oil pipeline Ust'-Balyk — Kurgan — Ufa — Al'metevsk	520.0	649.9
Oil pipeline Kuibyshev — Tikhoretskaya	143.5	267.0
Abakan rolling-stock factory	293.0	500.9
Tuvaasbest combine	43.2	91.9
Rybina printing equipment factory	25.5	44.2
Kostroma cylinder and piston factory	52.9	236.4

Source: Isaev, 1973, p. 33.

organisations can cover up other forms of escalation. A survey covering the period 1971-5 blamed design errors and increases in machinery prices, taken together, for almost a quarter of capital cost escalations (Dyker, 1983a, pp. 63-4). Given that the success-indicator regime has not presented strong inducements to cost sensitivity on the part of design organisations, this is perhaps not a surprising figure. In fact, however, cost-hike elements apparently directly related to the work of design organisations may on closer examination once again turn out to be rather a reflection of economy-wide tendencies.

'To get construction started at any cost, and that means having to prove that the given project is economically highly attractive — that is in many cases the unspoken behest to the design worker' (Perepechin and Apraksina, 1980). Ministries often put extreme pressure on design organisations to understate estimated capital costs, just so that a given project can be squeezed into the below-limit category. When Promstroiproekt (general industrial design organisation), for example, estimated the cost of the production block of Sibgipromez (specialist ferrous metallurgy design organisation) in Kemerevo at 5.2 million rubles, the Ministry of Ferrous Metallurgy simply cut this to 2.5 million rubles — the then limit — on confirmation. In the end the project cost 5.8 million rubles (Shavlyuk, 1979). This helps us to understand how intermediate planning bodies are able to pursue their organisational-autarkical aims with such persistence, but it is hardly fair to place the 'blame' on the shoulders of the design workers.

What about straightforward mistakes in design? There can be no doubt that the quantitatively oriented planning regime has tended to create a blasé attitude to errors amongst design workers. The fact that the estimated cost of the fenol-acetone and nitric acid departments of the Saratov chemical combine rose by 10.5 million rubles is clearly not unconnected with the 1,700 changes and corrections that had to be made to the design (Vovchenko, 1965, p. 25). Again, however, we have to be extremely careful about imputing blame. Kudashov, for instance, portrays 'corrections' in designs presented by construction organisations as basically a ploy by the latter to fuel their own quest for *val*.

> Here also: 'the dearer the better'. In any case, the last word . . . in the end always lies with the builder. And sometimes when it comes to the last word the designer may lose his voice altogether: construction organisations have created a powerful barrier on the road to reductions in estimates consisting of estimate-contractual and technical services whose role in the agreement of designs comes down in practical terms to a search for anything that will make construction more expensive. (Kudashov, 1983, p. 9)

We can confirm that the construction stage has been an independent source of inflationary pressures by looking at figures on material expenditures and wage costs. A survey of 1,587 construction organisations undertaken in 1960 by Stroibank revealed excessive utilisation of basic materials, in relation to norms, averaging 20 per cent. Evidence from more recent years suggests no substantial improvement in the position. Workers are sometimes paid anything up to quadruple time for doing illegal overtime on their official day off, and *shabashniki* – 'lump' workers – make 2–4 times the 'normal' wage in Western Siberia. Aggregate overspending of the wages fund for all the construction ministeries in 1975 was only 1.5 per cent, though it was over 3 per cent for some ministries. Much higher figures are, of course, reported for particular organisations (Dyker, 1983a, pp. 85-6). In any case, there is so much scope for *planned* wages fund to get out of step with the implications of overall cost plans that the significance of these figures should not be overstressed. Unit wage costs in relation to output in Eastern Siberia rose 10-20 per cent in a number of key construction organisations during 1975–82 (Bezdelev, 1983). Given that there must have been some capital-deepening in the organisations concerned over that period, while there has been no major adjustment of the general level of construction wage rates, a very considerable element of pure inflation must be present here.

In the past, wages fund planning, if we can call it that, has been based on a particularly crude application of the ratchet principle, with the annual fund being based on the previous year's actual wage expenditure, even if that was above plan ('Zarabotnaya plata . . .', 1968). From 1983 the wages fund is supposed to be planned on the basis of norms relating to planned volumes of work. The trouble with that idea is that different types of work vary in labour-intensity, and therefore require different wage-output norms. As long as construction output indicators remain as crude as we have seen they do, the scope for fiddling the planned wages fund by fiddling the 'assortment' of planned construction work remains unlimited (Bezdelev, 1983). At a more specific level, the system of tariffs which is supposed to keep piece-rate earnings more or less in line with a putative 'normal' wage for each grade of worker does not function properly. In 1979 the 'tariff' accounted for only 50-60 per cent of total earnings. This is apparently closely related to fiddling on the estimated wage costs of auxiliary work (Komarov, 1979). Lastly, bonus funds and regional supplement moneys are often abused (Dyker, 1983a, p. 85).

What are the roots of building-site inflation in the Soviet Union? Obviously, the success-indicator system does not encourage economising attitudes. More specifically, storming patterns induced by the tyranny of short-term output plans impel managers to take a cavalier attitude to costs. As we saw earlier, an average of nearly 50 per cent of housing completions was concentrated in the last quarter of the year over the period 1953-73. But in that quarter labour productivity normally falls to just 65-70 per cent of its normal level (Dyker, 1983a, pp. 94-5). This reflects the taking on of large numbers of additional workers, often of low calibre, but presumably at very good effective wage rates. Of course the intensity of storming patterns is conditioned as much by the milieu in which construction organisations operate as by their own planning regime, and much the same could be said of many of the other operational problems which manifest themselves at the actual construction stage. It is to that milieu that we now turn.

The Construction Industry and the Pattern of the Soviet Planning System

We have seen that supply uncertainty is an endemic characteristic of the over-centralised Soviet planning system. But supply uncertainty has affected construction so acutely that it merits specific treatment in the present context. To put the problem into general perspective: according to the Deputy Minister of Ministroi USSR the 1979 *plan* for deliveries to the ministry was 150 million rubles short of requirements. Taking into account the fact that not all planned deliveries arrive, the total gap was 200 million rubles, representing 4 per cent of the requirements of the annual plan. We must add considerably to this to take account of poor quality and misdirected deliveries, so that the overall picture of supply uncertainty in this particular case is very sharply delineated indeed.

Turning to more specific supplies, it has been remarked that building enterprises, despite the old proverb 'Do not cut off the branch you are sitting on,' seem to be particularly bad at building factories for the building materials industry. This point is graphically underlined by the figures in Table 5.3. In consequence, non-metal construction materials have often been in outright deficit. Some areas have been served better than others, and the network of establishments run by the Ministry for Building Materials itself is territorially extremely unevenly distributed. The Ministry has virtually nothing in north-western Siberia, the northeast, and some north-western provinces of the RSFSR. Nevertheless there are 35,000 construction materials establishments in the Soviet Union, and one might be tempted to cite excessively small scale as a cause of supply difficulties. The direction of causation does, in fact, tend to be in the opposite direction, with organisations building up their own 'dwarf-workshops' as a hedge against supply uncertainty. The officially reported number of building materials associations and independent enterprises in 1979 was just 3,864.

The situation with regard to steel deliveries and the supply of construction equipment has been similarly unsatisfactory. Even paint brushes have been a major bottleneck. Lastly, poor coordination of the delivery schedules of equipment for installation has often caused both delays in completion and accumulations of uninstalled equipment. Most obviously, supply uncertainty of these various types exacerbates the problem of excessive lead-times and generally lowers the quality of work, especially finishing work, thus fortifying a tendency already present for success-indicator reasons. But it also intensifies the cost problem. Poor quality and specification in supplies of gravel and sand result in a rate of above-normal utilisation of cement reaching 20 per cent. Additional labour expenditures on fitting reaching 70 per cent have been required in construction administration No. 28, a subdivision of Mosstroi-6 trust, in order to excise defects in ceiling slabs. Excessively early deliveries of equipment have an obvious cost

Table 5.3: Percentage Fulfilment of Plans for Construction of Enterprises Producing Non-metallic Building Materials

	1976	1977	1978
Ministry of Heavy Industrial Construction	22.8	46.2	73.9
Ministry of Industrial Construction	92.0	83.0	99.2
Ministry of Construction	84.2	69.3	67.8
Ministry of Transport Construction	57.2	89.6	84.2

Source: Lifatov, 1980, p. 21.

in terms of the implicit rate of interest, but in the absence of adequate storage facilities the costs can be much greater, as veritable scrap-heaps of valuable equipment accumulate on sites (Dyker, 1983a, pp. 88–91).

Why is the supply problem so especially bad in construction? Primarily, it seems, because of the ways in which ministries seek to safeguard flows of investment funds from the centre and ensure short-term plan fulfilment. We saw earlier that ministerial overbidding for investment votes is a major direct input into the problem of excessive lead-times. It also tends to create an extraordinarily high degree of tautness in construction organisation plans. Thus the overall output target set for Minstroi USSR in 1979 was 5,903 million rubles' worth of work. But the implications of the annual plan as a whole represented 6,945 million rubles' worth of work for the ministry. On top of that the ministerial ploy of starting projects before approval, as a way of applying pressure for approval, means that building organisations are often working on sites which have neither allocation certificates for supplies nor any guarantee that they will ever be completed.

Organisations endeavouring to safeguard their supplies through building up an autarkical position would naturally be concerned to acquire direct control over the purveyance of building services, and there can be no doubt that the production potential of the Soviet construction industry has been stunted by organisational fragmentation just as has that of design organisations. The Institute of Construction Economics estimates that the optimal size for primary building organisations correponds to an annual value of work greater than 1.5 million rubles, and on this basis over 60 per cent of such organisations were of sub-optimal size in 1960, during the *sovnarkhoz* period. The situation had, however, been worse under the old ministerial system, and it rapidly deteriorated when that system was reinstated in 1965. Odessa correspondents of *Pravda* noted in 1969 that in the four preceding years the number of building and building-maintenance organisations in the city had grown four times, with all the organisations being under different departments. Contemporary material suggests that the labour productivity lead of 'complex' construction associations over specialised (frequently departmental) trusts may be of the order of 100 per cent (Dyker, 1983a, p. 92). All this helps us to understand the paradox of a top-priority activity like investment apparently moving forward on something of a shoe-string at the level of the actual building site. It is because bureaucrats have perceived the necessity of over-bidding in the scramble for investment votes that supply to the building site has been such a problem. It is in turn because construction capacity has been seen as something too important to leave to the construction ministries that it has been prevented from developing on a concerted national pattern. Much the same thing can be said about the design sector.

If we place these factors side by side with the pressures of gross-output-based success-indicators we can hardly be surprised at the persistence of quality problems in Soviet construction, and in particular of perennial underachievement in relation to technology. The techno-logy of construction management is backward, with basic elements like critical path analysis still not fully assimilated, and even the level of basic bricks-and-mortar technology leaves a lot to be desired — pre-fabricated blocks, for example are still not widely used (Dyker, 1983a, pp. 86-7). But it is the quality and technological level of the finished investment project that really matters in this connection, and in turning our attention to that variable we implicitly pose a wider question: long lead-times and cost-hikes apart, just how sub-optimal is the return that the Soviet economy obtains in the end of the day from its investment effort?

Investment Planning and Investment Pay-offs

A *Pravda* editorial from 1974 noted that seven blast furnaces commis-sioned in 1973, plus the convertor departments of the Karaganda, Western Siberia and Chelyabinsk steel works, did not have automatic control systems, and censured designers for this. A report from 1978 blames conservatism on the part of design organisations in relation to new materials for excess capacity in new, advanced construction mater-ials factories (Dyker, 1983a, p. 57). This is rather unfair, since existing regulations in some cases forbid designers to use light construction materials, once again confirming that we are talking about a whole complex of planning problems, rather than just the sins of particular organisations. Specific defects in commissioned projects can often be laid more directly at the door of building organisations. Because finishing work produces less gross output than earlier stages, it tends to be systematically neglected. In Azerbaidzhan 'completed' schools have been left without running water or window glass, with unpainted walls and unfinished classrooms. New houses in Lithuania have lacked proper insulation, and the removal of a light switch can leave a hole right through to the next house. Gas pipeline builders in the Komi autonomous republic located in North European Russia, have neglected construction of compressor stations in favour of maximising the length of actual pipe laid, as the easiest way to fulfil output targets (in this case unofficial output targets set at the ministerial level). Pipeline capacity in the absence of compression is only 30–35 per cent what it should be (Dyker, 1983a, p. 84).

Yet there is an aspect to the question of pay-offs that is more fundamental than anything thrown up by these quaint success-indicator anecdotes. We saw in the first section of this chapter that formal Soviet investment appraisal criteria cannot present the planners with a unique array of desirable investment starts, even if they are used consistently. We observed in earlier chapters that to the extent that ministries and enterprises, etc. have had control over project choice they have tended to go for projects that would safeguard their own supply situation, rather than those that would come out top on the Present Value or any other general criterion. Just how often do the Russians put the wrong factory in the wrong place? We cannot hope to answer this question conclusively, but the attempt is worth while because it helps us to see how micro-economic issues tie in with some of the great developmental issues we broached earlier on.

There is an official list of Soviet 'principles of location of productive forces'. It runs as follows:

(1) Location of enterprises as near as possible to raw material sources and centres of consumption.
(2) Even distribution of economic activity throughout the country.
(3) Rational division of labour between economic regions, and complex development of the economy of each region.
(4) Raising of the economic and cultural level of all backward national areas to that of the most advanced.
(5) Elimination of the distinction between town and country.

(6) Strengthening of the defence potential of the country.
(7) International division of labour within the socialist bloc.

If we allow for a certain awkwardness of presentation, there is little here that would raise the eyebrows of a left-of-centre spatial planner in the West. Locational decisions should be made with due account taken of optimal transport patterns and regional natural advantages. At the same time matters of social justice and ethnic peace should quite properly be taken into consideration. Principles (2) and (5) go rather beyond that, but in fact they have been quietly dropped by Soviet writers on location in recent years (Dyker, 1983a, pp. 114–17). We would not, then, expect anything very abnormal in the way of spatial decisions to come out of the observance of the official locational principles. Once again, if we want to get to the nub of the matter, we have to look at the organisational picture.

As we saw earlier, there are two stages in the process of feasibility study in the Soviet Union. The 'development and location scheme', worked out for sectors and regions, aims to present an overall picture of likely directions of medium- and long-term development. Within this context feasibility studies proper (TEOs) are then elaborated for major individual projected investment starts. In practice this system has been extremely weak.

> The quality of schemes still does not meet contemporary require-
> ments. In many of them the 'point of departure' is not properly
> assessed, and the latest achievements of science and technology and
> other factors not taken into consideration . . . Multiple variants in
> terms of location and output levels, taking inter-sectoral links into
> account, are rare. (Shiryaev, 1977, p. 29)

Again:

> TEOs frequently do not go beyond the appraisal of the advisability of
> constructing separate enterprises or projects; they fail to take
> account of the development of complementary enterprises in allied
> sectors, necessary to guarantee projected capacities with raw mat-
> erial and energy resources, and with the facilities for further pro-
> cessing of output. ('Uporyadochit'. . .', 1965, p. 11)

The problem of inadequate TEOs was one of the main themes of the colloquium on design work held in Moscow in May 1974, and new regulations greatly increasing the stress on feasibility studies swiftly followed the recommendations of that colloquium. These new regulations proved, however, to be ineffectual, and the 1981 design decree returned to the problem. This time the approach was to abolish the TEO as such, and integrate its content back into an upgraded system of schemes (Dyker, 1983a, pp. 51-2, 67). That represented a commendable recognition of the interdependence of investment decisions, indeed an embodiment of locational principle (3), but the 1984 investment decree re-establishes the separateness of the TEO. Contemporary sources confirm that the problem of inadequate feasibility studies is as serious as ever. Why so?

Firstly, they are entrusted to design organisations or ministries. The latter, as we shall elaborate below, are very far from placing top priority on locational niceties. Ministerial penchants may also have been guilty in a less direct way. To the extent that it is departmentalism that has created the 'atomisation without specialisation' pattern which characterises the general structure of the design organisation system; (a) an appropriate specialised organisation may simply not exist in the case of a given project, and this will affect fundamental decisions more than it will the detailed working out of drawings, etc.; (b) a very large number of organisations may be working on the same project, which makes it extremely difficult for any one of them to cope adequately with general strategic questions, and indeed may leave it unclear who is responsible in this area. 'Thematic plans are confirmed late and often changed. Ministries chop and change the allocation of design projects, which makes stability in plans difficult' (Fedorenko and Yandovskii, 1976, p. 37). Equally important has been the tendency for early-stage work to be undervalued in terms of estimates of the total cost of a design, thus making it 'less advantageous'.

In some sectors of industry, and also with some large-scale construction projects, limits [i.e. on maximum expenditures – D.A.D.] for the compilation of technico-economic feasibility studies for development and location are for unknown reasons very much on the low side, which is often one of the reasons why design work and construction of projects is carried on without adequate economic foundation. (Khikmatov, 1969, p. 86).

Paralleling this, there is apparently no special financial provision for clients to pay for the elaboration of feasibility studies (Mironov, 1983).

The big problem with the 1981 provisions was, of course, that they actually increased the role of the ministries in this whole area, by increasing the status of the sectoral development and location scheme. A contemporary writer accuses the ministries of generally neglecting the schemes, and more specifically of being more interested in fiddling estimates, to get projects in as below-limit and to cover up cost-hikes, than in proper examination of locational issues (Kuz'mich, 1983). Inevitably, however, the 1984 resuscitation of the TEOs is to be organised by the ministries. Ministries, indeed, seem to have so much effective power over the investment process, and so many good departmental reasons for doing 'bad' things, that we may wonder, as indeed Khrushchev wondered as early as 1957, whether the whole system of administering investment in the Soviet Union has not been rather disastrous from the point of view of effectiveness. In Chapter 1 we argued, on an essentially macro-economic basis, that ministerial over-bidding for investment resouces and organisational autarky have to be seen as integral parts of the strategy of using fixed capital investment as a key instrument of resource mobilisation. Thus the functional defensibility of the former very much depends, in the first instance, on our assessment of the latter, and of its relevance to a particular period of Soviet economic development. Now we must expand on the meso- and micro-economic levels, and try to assess the impact of organisational patterns on regional development, and on individual projects.

Apart from inducing an 'abnormal' degree of labour-intensity, the main problem with the tendency to organisational autarky is that it distorts locational patterns, and may result in grossly excessive transport hauls.

> The ministries see the Irtysh steppe as just a site for enterprises. Having built the factories, they usually start to supply them from afar with 'their own' raw materials, though these are produced in adequate quantities in Pavlodar [local big town – D.A.D.] – but by other ministries. (Poltoranin and Sevest'yanov, 1977)

Transport organisations, still heavily oriented to gross-output-type success-indicators, have no incentive to minimise hauls, and in any case transport capacity is one of the things that ministries tend to 'collect'. An inspection in 1976 of nine provinces in the RSFSR, for example, revealed that over the previous two years departmental lorry parks had grown by a total of 470,000, while those of specialist transport organisations had grown by only 62,000, despite the fact that costs in the former are 1.2–2.3 times what they are in the latter (Sergienkov, 1976). Under the *sovnarkhoz* system the tendency to excessive toing and froing was halted, but localistic penchants produced, by contrast, a powerful tendency to 'duplicating capacities'. In Central Asia, for example, each of the four republics, to which the *sovnarkhozy* had been made co-extensive, built their own cable and general metal goods factories in the early *sovnarkhoz* period (subsequently a single Central Asian *sovnarkhoz* was created, precisely to counteract these tendencies) (Dyker, 1983a, p. 40). Thus under the regional economic councils less fuel was wasted on cross-hauls, but more potential economies of scale were passed over.

We should note, however, that intermediate-level organisational autarky does lead to sacrifice of economies of scale under the ministerial systems as well. Because ministries have to operate mainly within the framework of the existing pattern of enterprises, because their effective independence is largely restricted to real or bogus reconstruction of existing plants, they are not in a position fully to 'rationalise' their autarkical preferences. Engineering Ministry X might well prefer to supply all its Moscow main-activity factories with components from a single components factory under its jurisdiction, and located in Moscow itself. But unless it is lucky enough to have inherited such a plant, it will have to look further afield for capacities 'suitable' for ancillary production lines. The outlying regions of the Soviet Union have their frameworks of small engineering plants, often originally built up with local needs, especially maintenance needs, in mind. The ministries have notoriously tended to distort these local complexes away from their original purpose, and to press them into service as components shops for national production complexes. This pattern can be seen very clearly in, for example, the case of the engineering industry in Tadzhikistan, the most peripheral of the Central Asian republics (Dyker, 1983a, pp. 150–7). The conclusion is inescapable that it is the peculiar half-way house of Soviet investment planning – neither properly centralised nor properly decentralised – that makes organisational autarky such a wasteful phenomenon. We are talking here about the way things are and always have been, rather than any movement towards change. Nevertheless there is striking confirmation of the general principle that emerged from Chapter 3, viz. that attempts to mix specific bits of centralisation and decentralisation against the background of a generally high degree of centralisation (which is what ultimately conditions organisational autarky) is bad news.

So much for internal economies of scale. When we come to consider *external* economies of scale, economies which accrue as the build-up of agglomerations reduces transport costs and makes for a secular upward trend in labour productivity among regional labour forces, the case is a little different. The ministerial penchant for long cross-hauls has certainly prejudiced the interests of complex development, and ministries have been markedly unwilling to push investment into labour-surplus rural areas and small towns where it may be presumed that productivity prospects are long-term rather than medium-term. In the case of Central Asia, where, with birth rates still very high, rural labour surpluses are much more significant than in other parts of the Soviet Union, they stand accused of taking the attitude that 'Uzbekistan [is] . . . reducible to a single point – Tashkent' (Zakirov, 1965, p. 67). The Gas and Oil Ministries have likewise been pilloried for failing to develop infrastructure and build up a stable local force in Western Siberia (Dyker, 1983a, pp. 157–74). But at the level of regional development the authorities have in many cases been able to mobilise a sufficient counterweight to departmentalist tendencies. The record in Siberia is patchy, with the integrated development of the Urals-Kuzbass combine contrasting with a West Siberian experience which has shown Gosplan in a rather weak and helpless light. In Eastern Siberia giant hydro-electric stations completed in the 1960s and 1970s have permitted the development of an integrated power-intensive industrial complex, though departmentalism was partly to blame for substantial excess capacity in early years (Dyker, 1983a, pp. 119–33). In Central Asia one can draw a sharp contrast between the messiness of location patterns at the plant-by-plant level, especially in engineering, and the considerable successes recorded at the level of the region as a whole. Starting from a situation *c.* 1930 characterised by an almost complete absence of industry, but the existence of a fairly developed cotton cash-crop agriculture, the Soviet authorities demonstrated the strength of their *sui generis* capital-ample approach with substantial and sustained capital transfers into the region, invested mainly in agriculture, irrigation, education and agriculture-related light industry. Industrial labour productivity in Central Asia as a whole still appears to be lower than the national average, and the regional economy remains less integrated than locational principle (3) demands. But Moscow must gain fairly high marks in the Central Asian case for maintaining a balance of specialisation and regional self-sufficiency, at least at the inter-sectoral level, sometimes in the face of some opposition from departmental and local interests.

The power of centralised command has been demonstrated not only in the positive form of providing impetus for complex development in pioneer areas. However much we may suspect that the central Soviet authorities themselves may have indulged in particular kinds of 'investment good fetishism', they appear to have been fairly successful in preventing local political establishments doing the same. There are exceptions, and the giant Nurek hydro-electric station, built to a capacity of 2.7 million kilowatts in mountain-bound Tadzhikistan with no clear idea at the time of who was going to use the electricity, is an outstanding one (Dyker, 1983a, pp. 140–50). But that scheme was pushed through during the *sovnarkhoz* period, when the regionalisation of industrial administration undoubtedly increased the political leverage of local political cadres. What we can say with confidence is that state investment in the Soviet Union has not been systematically distorted by local pressures for prestige projects, job-creation, etc. Of course the decayed industrial area is a treat still in store for the Soviet planners, while the emergence of serious regional concentrations of unemployment is unlikely to happen until the pressure generally to raise labour productivity finally becomes irresistible. Thus the planning system may face sterner tests in this connection in the future than it has in the past.

Finally in this section, we must say a word about production externalities. Predictably, ministries and enterprises have a bad record on pollution, and the Caspian Sea and Lake Baikal have been seriously damaged by industrial excesses. Because a proper transfer price for land is not charged in the Soviet Union, a whole category of costs which are mainly internalised in Western market economies are exteranlised in the Soviet Union. For instance, the proposed construction of a mid-Yenisei hydro-electric station at Abalakovo, Eastern Siberia, controversial but heavily promoted by the Energy Ministry, would submerge large volumes of high-quality timber and a considerable amount of valuable agricultural land, including market garden areas (Dyker, 1983a, pp. 46–8). Some progress has been made in recent years towards closer central control in relation to this problem, but the continued failure of the Soviet authorities to introduce a generalised framework of rental payments, for land or exhaustible resources never mind other less concrete resources, has been a major obstacle to the development of any kind of system of automatic penalising of polluters. Given that the introduction of interest payments was a major element of the 1965 planning reform, and given that the trend since then has been to try to increase the sensitivity of the planning system to cost variables, we may speculate on the nature of the sticking-point

Table 5.4: Soviet Incremental Capital-Output Ratios (ICORs), 1966–83

1966–70	3.5	1979	13.3
1971–5	5.2	1980	7.4
1976	5.0	1981	8.8
1977	6.5	1982	7.2
1978	6.2	1983	7.3

Sources: Various editions of ECE, *Economic Survey of Europe*.

in relation to rent. Of course with the big industrial ministries dominating the premium sites in the cities, the immediate effect of the introduction of systematic rents would be to make a terrible mess of balance sheets. Even if the ministries were thereby induced to modify their locational attitudes, systematic adjustments would probably have to be made throughout the price system. Ministerial vested interest may have been a major independent factor holding up developments in this area.

In looking more closely at project choice in the Soviet Union we have largely confirmed the picture that emerged from a consideration of the problems of costs and excessive lead-times. External economies of scale and political toughness apart, the micro-economics of Soviet investment planning is as bad as the macro-economics. This does not provide an explanation for the downward trend in Soviet capital productivity, except to the extent that we can argue that these various problems have actually been getting worse. There is, certainly, evidence that the average lead-time actually lengthened in the 1970s (Dyker, 1983a, p. 36) but the dramatic trend illustrated in Table 5.4 can hardly be explained in this way. Rather that trend reflects the resource availability factors discussed earlier, especially in relation to energy supplies, and perhaps some intensification of the general planning problem, as the economy has become bigger and more complex. But there is clearly some sense in which the Soviet Union has been able in the past to 'afford' specific weaknesses in investment planning, and can no longer do so. Looking at it more optimistically, there is substantial scope on the organisational side to make up some of the ground lost in relation to investment effectiveness for largely 'objective' reasons.

The Investment Bank and the Construction Committee – How Much Difference do they Make?

We have emphasised the sense of lacuna in Soviet investment planning, the extent to which an excessive burden of short-term planning makes it impossible for Gosplan to pay proper attention to the medium and long term. But the investment/construction complex does have its own specialised planning bodies. Gosstroi USSR (State Committee of the USSR Council of Ministers for Construction Affairs) was created on 9 May 1950. Stroibank (Investment or Construction Bank) was created on 7 April 1959, taking over the competences of a number of specialised banks, including the Agricultural and Industrial Banks. Thus the final stages of the period of extensive growth were marked by attempts at concentration in the field of investment planning and finance.

Organs of *ekspertiza* (design monitoring organisations) are normally subordinate to USSR or republican Gosstroi, and these have the right to reject projects outright on general efficiency grounds. All the evidence suggests, however, that this does not happen very often, and when it does happen the determined minsterial administrator may be more than a match for his colleagues in *ekspertiza*. When, for example, Glavgosekspertiza (Main State *ekspertiza*) recently threw out the design for a building materials factory on the grounds that two existing factories of the same type had shown disappointing results, the ministry simply changed tack, and submitted designs for *two* similar factories in different areas. The lowest level of *ekspertiza* organ is, in fact, actually subordinate to the ministry rather than to Gosstroi, so that very little could be expected of it at the strategic decision-taking level. On the more detailed level *ekspertiza* organs are charged with seeing that standard designs and financial norms are observed, and that costs are kept down and proper measures taken to raise effectiveness. Designs are sometimes thrown out at this stage on grounds of technical obsolescence, and *ekspertiza* often manages to get estimates down a little. But here again the general opinion of the effectiveness of the monitoring organs is fairly low. It is clear that *ekspertiza* have neither the resources nor the clout to make a substantial difference to the overall level of investment effectiveness.

The picture is similar in relation to another member of the Gosstroi family, the State Operationalisation Commission. As noted earlier, the Commission had, prior to 1966, so very formal a remit that it had little chance to be effective. Since then a consistent effort has been made to give more strength to its elbow, without, it appears, a great deal of success. Complaints about its ineffectuality are still common, and one *cause célèbre* reported in *Pravda* concerned the signing of an operationalisation certificate for a factory that did not exist. New legislation aims to tighten up procedures still further, but purely procedural changes will surely continue to run up against a number of powerful factors tending to neutralise the *raison d'être* of the Commission. First, although individual commissions are ultimately responsible to Gosstroi, they tend to be dominated in practice by local and departmental interests, certainly in relation to run-of-the-mill projects. Secondly, the traditional orientation of the whole system towards short-term output maximisation means that there is always pressure to pass a project, so that it can start to produce *something*. Lastly, formal operationalisation means a reduction in officially reported unfinished construction, which is, of course, pure virtue.

Gosstroi itself is much concerned with legislation, promulgating building regulations, revising norms, etc., and there are frequent reports of it getting behind with this work. That may provide the key to an understanding of the comparative ineffectuality of the whole Gosstroi system in relation to investment effectiveness. Thus the argument cited above in relation to Gosplan, namely that the burden of routine work makes any kind of longer-term perspective impossible, seems to apply almost equally to Gosstroi.

Stroibank shares with *ekspertiza* the right to veto dubious projects, and this right has been exercised systematically. In addition the bank can withhold finance to projects not furnished with the requisite design and financial documentation. Cost-paring work by Stroibank has produced economies of over 20 per cent in some cases, though on average economies achieved come to just about 1 per cent of total estimated value. The bank has been criticised for concerning itself less with the quality aspects of design work. Construction organisations are obliged to submit to Stroibank annual intra-project title lists (*vnutripostroechnyi titul'nyi spisok*) which permit monitoring of costs and gestation periods, and form the basis for planning the amount of short-term credit needed to finance unfinished construction. It is not uncommon for projects to be excluded from intra-project title lists because of inadequate financial cover. As with designs, the general impression is that Stroibank is a more effective monitor of construction work in relation to costs than in relation to quality factors. But this may be changing, and there have been cases of funds being withheld from construction ministries in connection with poor quality work. Overall, Stroibank seems to be a somewhat more muscular inspection organisation than Gosstroi, though it has been suggested that this may reflect a bias in the sources (Green, 1984). In any case, neither body is able to do more than marginally modify the general tendencies discussed in this chapter (Dyker, 1983a, pp. 48–50, 69–71, 96–8).

It was no doubt very much with these weaknesses of planning and control in mind that Gosplan decided in 1982 to create a 'Unified Investment Planning System', ESPKS, based on an integrated information base containing design characteristics and parameters of all projects. The system is designed to help Gosplan itself, Gosstroi and Stroibank to shift the emphasis in their work from ex-post *criticism* to ex-ante *planning* and continuous monitoring (Bulgakov, 1983). This is certainly a step in the right direction, but at the given level of centralisation the burden placed on Soviet computer technology must be staggering.

6 THE FUTURE OF THE SOVIET ECONOMIC PLANNING SYSTEM

We have spent five chapters taking the Soviet planning system to pieces, putting it into historical perspective, and pin-pointing its main weaknesses. In essaying now to formulate ways in which it might be changed and improved, in the context of the tasks and constraints of the moment, we encounter two main difficulties. The first is the political dimension, which has surely been at least as important in determining the course of economic reform in the Soviet Union as any technological imperatives. The second is the inherent difficulty of charting speculative courses of further economic reform on an essentially *a priori* basis. No attempt will in fact be made to bring the political dimension into the analysis on a systematic basis, but we will try to expand on some of our earlier asides in this connection. As far as the second problem is concerned, we will try to bring a greater empirical element into our speculations by referring to the experience of some of the smaller countries within the Soviet bloc which have indeed already tried out some of the things that the Russians may be thinking of trying out.

Let us start by jumping in at the deep end. The system of collective and state farms set up by Stalin in the 1930s has been, for the Soviet Union at least, a disaster from the point of view of production and a near-disaster from that of productivity. In particular the effort sustained through the 1970s and early 1980s by the Soviet authorities to spend their way out of trouble in agriculture has failed utterly. Vast investments have produced next to no return, and improved remuneration has produced no sharp upward movement in general levels of X-efficiency. It is perfectly proper to point to the particularly bad run of weather conditions in the late 1970s, but it is equally in order to ask why colossal inputs into drainage and irrigation schemes have not done more to stabilise harvests, and why the system appears simply to lack the kind of motivational impetus and flexibility required to get farmers out in the middle of the night to save weather-threatened crops in the way that is more or less routine on family farms in Western Europe.

Certainly, the currently fashionable Hungarian agricultural system lays no special stress on work-team independence, but this should be seen against the background of Hungarian geographical and historical conditions. Hungary is almost all plain, and the agricultural environment varies little from one region to another. Rainfall conditions and the hardness of the winter are closer to what we know in Western Europe than to what the Soviet Union commonly experiences. It is quite simply much easier to grow things in Hungary than it is in the Soviet Union, and the 'loving care' element which explains so much of the difference, even for very ordinary crops, in performance between Soviet state/collective and private sectors is merely important, rather than absolutely crucial, in gentler climes. Production of specialist lines is, of course, highly concentrated in the private sector in Hungary. Pre-1918 Hungary was largely organised in *latifundia*, and while peasant proprietorship was a political issue, it never became a widespread and lasting reality. Partly, perhaps, for this reason, but also because of the special conditions prevailing in post-1956 Hungary, collectivisation was pushed through fairly painlessly. In contemporary Hungary working on a state farm or cooperative does not set you apart from the rest of society in the way that the equivalent status in the Soviet Union still does, and while Hungarian economists may wonder whether some of the very big farms might not profitably be broken up into smaller units, the basic organisational set-up does not seem to be an issue. In the Soviet Union, by contrast, the issue of how work-teams should be organised is so very sensitive because behind it lurks the ultimate question of whether the *sine qua non* of any effective reform of agricultural planning might not be the abolition of the system of state and collective farms.

But that, says the Communist Party apparatus man, is politically impossible, and he may be right in the sense that retreat from an institution as old as the socialist enterprise might do irreparable damage to the credibility of the regime. It is precisely for this reason, however, that we may speculate that not every Party conservative is opposed to the most radical variants of the link system. All the evidence indicates that watered-down versions of the system do not work particularly well, do not revolutionise productivity. It is rather the hectarers and their like who seem to offer Soviet socialist agriculture some real prospect for intensification. And of course the more radical the approach to the work-team issue within the socialist sector, the more scope there is for fruitful cooperation between that sector and the private sector of the kind which we described in Chapter 4. Thus if the crucial political requirement is to save face by saving the formal framework of the *sovkhoz/kolkhoz* system then there is really no problem.

After all, even under the hectarer system there is still plenty of scope for a division of labour that would leave manuring, irrigation and spraying to the central farm management, even if the system were taken to its logical conclusion and choice of crop pattern decentralised to the hectarer as well. The collective farm remains a symbol of exploitation and alienation to the Soviet peasant, but it would surely not be beyond the wit of planners to design a system which shifted the focus of day-to-day operations away from the *sovkhoz* or *kolkhoz* to such an extent as to neutralise its symbolic importance to the peasant while retaining it for the political establishment.

Let us assume, then, that the authorities have decided to give the radical interpretation of the link its head, and to follow the Hungarian model in relation to farm-centre relationships by abolishing the procurement target as such and switching to an essentially parametric planning system in which prices would play the main role. This brings us back to the key problem which was introduced at the end of Chapter 4. If farming is to be marketised, what is to be done about the sectors of industry which are supplied by agriculture and which supply agriculture? The conclusion is inescapable that a positive approach to the agricultural planning problems must ultimately imply the marketisation of large areas of Soviet light industry, engineering and chemicals. After looking at just one key sector, then, we are already a long way towards suggesting that the Soviet planning authorities need to retreat once again to the Leninist 'commanding heights' of the economy, if they are to grapple seriously with fundamental problems of the system. Let us pursue this proposition.

Hungarian agriculture may be top of the class, but when it comes to the planning system as a whole it is unlikely that the Hungarian New Economic Mechanism would be adopted lock stock and barrel by any future Soviet leadership. Sheer political conservatism apart, a Soviet leader would surely consider that the record of centralised command planning in the Soviet military/industrial complex was rather good (Hungary, of course, does not have a large military/industrial complex) – but of this more later on. Going beyond that, it is unlikely that any future Soviet government would lightly sacrifice the relative price stability that has characterised the Soviet economy (in Hungary retail prices increased by an average of 6–7 per cent per annum from 1976 to 1983 (Economic Commission for Europe, 1984, Table 3.5.5). By the same token the present Soviet leadership must surely feel that the difficulties Hungary has recently been experiencing in trying to service and fund its 8 billion dollar foreign debt present a salutary lesson. The argument of Hungarian economists in the late 1960s and early 1970s was, of course, that Hungary, as a small, resource-poor country constrained to trade a very large proportion of its GNP, had no choice but to open itself up to the vagaries of the world price system and the risks attached to a more open system of foreign trade planning (Csikos-Nagy, 1978). By the early 1980s they could add that nearly all the smaller East European countries were in any case in foreign payments difficulties, market-socialist or not. For the Soviet Union, by contrast, the sheer size and resource endowment of the country continues to make a high degree of national autarky possible without paying too high a price. For the same reason Soviet economists have argued that it is neither feasible nor appropriate for the Soviet Union simply to take world prices as the basis for domestic. Again, Hungary's geographical compactness and homogeneity of population, coupled with the extreme degree of labour shortage felt throughout the post-war period, has meant that the introduction of the NEM in that country has brought with it no serious threat of unemployment. A Soviet leadership might well suppose that the market-socialist experience of Yugoslavia, with its ethnic diversity and cultural barriers, might be more relevant to the Soviet Union in this connection. In 1982 there were 808,623 officially registered unemployed in Yugoslavia, representing 8–9 per cent of the total active population, including the self-employed ('Višak nezaposlenih . . .', 1982).

Given all this, it is not surprising that the present Soviet leadership appears to be looking more in the direction of East Germany and Bulgaria in its search for alternative models of industrial planning. Quite apart from their more cautious approach to planning reform, those are the two countries of Eastern Europe which have stood up best in terms of growth trends to the difficult circumstances of the late 1970s and early 1980s. Bulgaria's reported growth rates are still in the 4–5 per cent per annum range, and the drop to 3 per cent in 1983 was purely a reflection of a substantial fall in agricultural production, conditioned by unfavourable weather factors. East Germany has reported growth rates of around 4 per cent since 1979, after a sticky period in the middle-late 1970s (Economic Commission for Europe, 1984, Table 3.1.1). Recalculations of these indices in GNP terms might well produce more modest figures, but one can say the same about all the other East European countries.

Both Bulgaria and East Germany significantly modified their planning systems in 1979, with the Bulgarians proclaiming a New Economic Mechanism. While these modifications are still very much within the mainstream of Soviet-type planning, they have clearly in turn had a substantial effect on reform thinking in the Soviet Union. A theme common to both countries, and echoed in Andropov's experimental industrial planning decree, is that of cutting the ministries down to size. In the Bulgarian NEM the traditional role of the ministries in plan implementation has been largely transferred to the association, combine or enterprise, leaving the ministry as a budget-financed organisation mainly concerned with medium-term matters, in particular investment and technical progress. Production organisations make no payments to ministries at all (Kirov, 1983, p. 120). In East Germany the new system is based on the combine, a conglomerate of related enterprises. Combines contrast with the associations, or VVBs (Vereinigungen Volkseigener Betriebe) they replace by being business rather than administrative bodies, and by being organised on the basis of vertical rather than horizontal integration. While the ministries retain substantial directive powers, subject to the principle of compensation where the financial position of a combine is injured, and a major role in basic production planning, combine managements are conceded decision-taking pre-eminence in a number of areas which have classically been the prerogative of the ministry or its administrative subordinate. In particular, the combine director can make decisions on shifting equipment around, opening new departments, and hiring and firing junior management (Melzer, 1981; Boot, 1983).

Much more important is what happened in the East German and Bulgarian models to the position of the enterprise/association/combine *vis-à-vis* the central planners. In Bulgaria the new principle is that production organisations should be wholly self-financing. The Soviet experimental industrial planning decree predicates, as we saw, an increase in the weight of enterprise funds and in management's rights to their autonomous disposition. But while that simply means more (effectively) decentralised investment, the dispositions of the Bulgarian NEM mean that *all* investment is financed from production organisation funds, major new capacities or technologies excepted. In addition, for the bulk of projects involving lead-times of less than three years no specific approval from centre or ministry is required, and no specific financial limits are imposed. Production organisations are conceded the right of free contract in relation to association or cooperative agreements with other organisations. In East Germany the principle of free contracting within the framework of the plan has been taken a good deal further, and supply contracts are in the first instance negotiated by the combines and other organisations involved, through the medium of so-called 'complex meetings', though subsequently subject to approval by ministry and government. Such combines are even allowed to negotiate foreign trade contracts independently (Boot, 1983, pp. 332–6). There is some echo of this approach to the problem of earning hard currency in the Bulgarian NEM provision for an enterprise hard currency own fund, though this does not appear to be backed up by any formalised degree of autonomy on export contracts (Kirov, 1983, p. 125).

Most important of all, what happens under these new arrangements to the output target? In East Germany the principle seems to be to maintain a substantial dimension of central directive in relation to output planning, irrespective of the degree of flexibility on contracts, but with the combines left to do a good deal of the 'balancing' calculations on which output targets must ultimately be based. In Bulgaria the key innovation in this area is the principle that obligatory output targets should henceforward represent essentially minimal rather than maximal figures. Beyond that Bulgarian enterprises are now to be allowed to formulate counterpart plans on a voluntary basis, in accordance with contracts signed for deliveries of above-plan production. Shortfalls on basic plan assignments for a given year are merely added in to the counterpart plan for the following year (Kirov, 1983, pp. 122–3). I believe that this represents the first attempt fully to formalise the principle of 'slack' planning in a Soviet-type system. There are powerful echoes here of the ways in which the Soviet reformers of the 1960s thought that a substantial decentralised investment dimension could be integrated into a centrally planned economy, and a sharp contrast with the provision of the 1979 Soviet planning decree which declared that counterpart plans, once agreed, should from then on be counted as part of the official plan for purposes of assessment of plan fulfilment. And however interested the present Soviet leadership may be in Bulgaria, we should note that the rule in Andropov's experimental industrial planning decree whereby managers should receive no bonuses at all unless sales/delivery plans are met — a decisive reassertion of the classic Micawber principle — is in the spirit of the Soviet 1979 decree, not that of the Bulgarian NEM.

While trends in East Germany and Bulgaria in relation to organisational patterns and fund-forming rules have, then, been similar to those visible in the Soviet Union, trends in the instruments and tactics of planning itself have not. There seem to be two major reasons for this. Most obviously, the re-emergence in the Soviet Union of some of the tactics of taut planning in recent years has surely represented a panic reversion to elements of the crude growth maximisation strategy in the face of steadily falling growth rates. East Germany, of course, was an industrialised country with a serious labour shortage and virtually no indigenous raw materials right from the start. This meant that resource mobilisation was not an issue, so that the problem of the balance of tautness/slackness as such has probably never had the kind of significance it has had in the Soviet Union. Certainly the central planning authorities in East Germany see it as their task to ensure that pressure for the fulfilment of medium-term growth targets is kept up, and this pressure may force ministries to override combine contractual commitments (Boot, 1983, p. 334). But the East German system is based on the principles of formal as well as informal negotiation, and its less holistic approach to some extent allows 'uncomfortable moments' to be routinised. This permits the ultimate degree of tautness to emerge out of a process of concertation from which the power of centralised command, is, of course, not absent. Counterpart planning was, in fact, abolished altogether in East Germany in 1980 (Knyazev, 1983, p. 124).

In Bulgaria, by contrast, the scenario has been very much one of a developing country, with a level of GNP per head one-fifth the US level in 1955, rising to one-third in 1965 (Economic Commission for Europe, 1980, p. 15), where crude growth-maximising tactics might have been expected to be fairly effective, if constrained by the smallness of the country. Certainly reported growth rates up to around 1980 were uniformly and substantially above 5 per cent per annum. Certainly Bulgarian economic policies have been characterised as recently as the mid-1970s by elements which could reasonably be described as 'impossible', for instance planned reduction in average lead-times in manufacturing and agriculture to 1–2 years (Economic Commission for Europe, 1977b, p. 98). Yet the transition to slack planning at the enterprise level is clearly confirmed by the recent pattern of planned and achieved growth rates in national income. With a planned rate of growth of 3.6 per cent 1982 was the first year since the introduction of Soviet-type planning for which a rate of growth of less than 5 per cent had been envisaged. In the event, a growth rate of 4.0 per cent was recorded. Despite this substantial degree of overfulfilment the target for 1983 was just 3.8 per cent (Economic Commission for Europe, 1983, p. 104). Thus the transition to slack planning in Bulgaria has clearly anticipated any secular downward trend in growth rates, has in fact aimed to engineer just such a downward trend, but with ample compensation envisaged in terms of the 'quality' of growth.

In the present context it is neither possible nor necessary to give a final verdict on the success of the Bulgarian NEM. But the Bulgarians have not found themselves, as have the Russians, between the Scylla and Charybdis of falling growth rates and inadquate quality perform- ance. Of course crude growth maximisation does not work in a complex industrial economy. But the short-term price of introducing explicit slackness into the Soviet planning system could certainly be near-zero growth rates for a couple of years. The more comforting medium-term prospect is emphasised by the fact that over the past twenty years East Germany's growth rate has, apart from the dip in the late 1970s, hardly varied at all.

'Nerve' is not, however, the only problem facing the Soviet planners in relation to their East European model options. Bulgarian GNP is no more than 3–4 per cent of Soviet. East German national income might reach a level of just about 10 per cent of that of its patron and ally. This dimension of scale becomes crucially important when we look at some of the more technical characteristics of the Bulgarian NEM. Given that that system does not involve a radical decentralisation of basic output planning as such, is there not a danger that fear of the ratchet will incline managers of production organisations to play safe in the traditional way, to fulfil their obligatory targets, and do just enough in the direction of counterpart planning to keep the politicians happy? As we saw in Chapter 2, the ratchet principle represents an element in growth strategy, but more fundamentally a response to the special technical problems of large, over-centralised systems, in terms of both information and consistency. In the small shows of Eastern Europe there is surely a strong *a priori* argument that once crude growth maxi- misation goes, as it has most emphatically under the Bulgarian NEM, there is no powerful technical reason why the ratchet principle should survive, even if systems remain fairly highly centralised. No detailed statistics to back up this argument have come to hand from Bulgaria itself, but it is most striking that in East Germany, a country which has been rather more cautious than the Bulgarians in relation to planning reform, the central planners compute balances for no more than around 300–400 commodity groups, with an additional 600–700 done by the ministries, and all the rest left to the combines themselves (Boot, 1983, p. 336). Bearing in mind Granick's conclusions, as quoted in Chapter 2, on the apparent absence of the ratchet in centre-ministry relations in the Soviet Union, would we really expect GDR central planners to feel heavily dependent on the ratchet at that level of work- load?

While this is good news for the East Germans and Bulgarians, however, it is bad news for conservative Soviet leaders hoping to import painless planning reform from loyal allies. To reduce the number of commodity groups planned at the centre in the Soviet Union from 15,000 to 300 would imply a decentralisation on a scale never contemplated in either East Germany or Bulgaria. But if that is the condition for getting rid of the ratchet principle once and for all, it is also, as was argued in Chapter 3, the condition for integrating wholly marketised sectors or subsectors of the economy into a general system which retains significant elements of centralised, command planning. In the light of what we have just said about agriculture, the importance of this point can hardly be exaggerated. The interim conclusion, then, is that the full rationalisation of the Soviet planning system would unavoidably take it so far along the road of both particular and general autonomisation of economic activity as to leave it almost unrecognisable.

There *are* certainly lessons for the Soviet Union in the planning theory and practice of these other two countries. In particular Bulgarian and East German experience has shown that the complementarity of centralised material balance planning, universal obligatory output targets and centrally imposed contracts, as in the traditional Soviet package, is not nearly so strict as Soviet planners may have supposed. More specifically, it seems perfectly possible to combine substantial decentralisation of material balancing to vertically integrated associations/combines with the maintenance of fairly detailed output targets *and* a substantial degree of freedom of contract. With that package many output targets must, of course, become in a sense voluntary, because the balances have been worked out by the organisation that is to be set the target. Equally important, output targets could get seriously out of line with contracts unless levels of organisational efficiency were fairly even between producing units to start off with.

Even here, then, a question-mark is raised over the exportability of East European approaches to the Soviet Union. There must surely be a fair number of enterprises in the Soviet Union which would have difficulty in obtaining *any* orders if systematic freedom of contract were permitted. That state of affairs partly reflects the size and regional heterogeneity of the country. It also reflects the strength of the emphasis on extensive growth in the past, with marginal or extramarginal enterprises hardly ever being closed down. No doubt, under contemporary conditions, the Soviet economy would ultimately be the stronger for getting rid of some of those establishments. But the transition period would again be extremely painful, in both output and employment terms. Once more we are arguing that any comfort Soviet leaders may take from the success of some small East European countries in finding a relatively smooth path to a viable half-way house on planning reform is illusory. However different the conditions in Hungary and in the Soviet Union, the latter does surely stand in need of the decisive radicalism of the Magyar approach of 1968.

But under whose tutelage, we must now ask, are the Russians to unlearn the bad habits of their traditional approach to investment planning? If we take the problem of excessive investment spread — *raspylenie sredstv* — as being fundamental and typical, we can proceed by trying to establish just what you have to do to get rid of it. We begin by attempting an exhaustive list of the factors which may condition the problem:

(1) Capital may be wholly or partly a free good.
(2) In a bureaucratic set-up, the more projects started in period 1, the easier it is to get more investment funds in period 2.
(3) Managers negotiating with planning authorities or banks will tend to discover that 'it is a typical feature . . . that the existing resource shares exert a considerable influence on future allocations' (Cave and Hare, 1981, p. 152). Any 'writing-off' therefore weakens a negotiator's position.
(4) Gestation periods are bound to be adversely affected by any tendency to supply uncertainty.
(5) Where there is endemic supply uncertainty in the given economy, clients and building organisations may wish to hedge against it by keeping open as many finishable options as possible.
(6) To the extent that enterprises are permitted to accumulate special funds for own investment, they may feel anxious to spend these accumulations as quickly as possible: (a) in case a future change of policy results in partial or total 'confiscation'; (b) to reduce the possibility of such a change occurring, by demonstrating that they are capable of using the funds.
(7) Elements of organisational inefficiency at design and construction stages may exacerbate this, as any other, problem of investment effectiveness.

We have seen all of those factors at work in the Soviet case — it is perhaps worth just noting apropos of (6), that quite apart from implications for the planning system as a whole, the saga of decentralised investment in the 1970s must have been a major factor in the worsening investment spread situation at that time, as the whole investment front was disorganised. The really interesting thing, however, is that in Hungary, where radical planning reform has largely excised factors (4), (5) and (7), the problem is still at least as bad as it is in the Soviet Union. An investigation published in the mid-1970s indicated that big projects often take over nine years to complete in Hungary (Szász, 1974), and it has been suggested that in the 1970s average lead-times in that country were significantly longer than in other socialist countries (Economic Commission for Europe, 1978, p. 140). On the basis of incomplete information the Secretariat of the Economic Commission for Europe suggest tentatively that 'little improvement in reducing gestation periods has taken place since 1980' (Economic Commission for Europe, 1983, p. 182). Hare concludes that

> the reform failed to convince enterprises that investment must be profitable, and that construction periods must be as expeditious as possible in the interests of efficiency. Central agencies also persisted in undertaking projects seen as 'necessary' given economic balances prepared in quantity terms. (Hare, 1983, p. 314)

The reasons for this appear to be essentially threefold. First, capital remains a very cheap good, if not an outrightly free one, even at the level of formal credit and interest arrangements. Enterprise investment accounts for over 60 per cent of total industrial investment in Hungary (Hare, 1979, p. 3), but a significant proportion of that 60 per cent represents grants and credits, often extended at very low effective interest rates (Cave and Hare, 1981, pp. 153–4). In addition, the absence of a capital market as such means that enterprises have little alternative but to spend own funds on own investment. It is not surprising in that context that factors (3) and (6) have exerted substantial pressure on the investment balance in Hungary. The degree to which that pressure has manifestly got through to the investment front itself in turn reflects the fact that the political economy of Hungary continues to be characterised by an extreme reluctance to force extra-marginal enterprises into bankruptcy. 'While formally possible under the 1970 enterprise statute, the procedures [for liquidation – D.A.D.] have almost never been invoked, except in the form of merging a failing enterprise with a more successful one' (Hare, 1983, p. 327). With no effective bankruptcy procedure, there is a sense in which *all* capital investment funds remain ultimately free.

We can sharpen the issues involved here if we move the spotlight to a country where the market-socialist approach has been entrenched more deeply and longer than anywhere inside the Soviet sphere of influence. Though 51 per cent of total investment in Yugoslavia was financed from credit in 1976–80 (Petrasinović, 1980), the total number of projects in progress at the end of 1978 was 31,335, as compared to 15,712 at the beginning of 1976 (Vlaho, 1979a). By March 1979 the total number had been reduced to 27,969, but there was still a gap of 15 billion dinars between available and required investment finance (Vlaho, 1979b). While no explicit figures on average lead-times in Yugoslavia have come to hand, they are certainly considered to be excessive (Koprivica, 1979). Of the 52 projects worth more than 500 million dinars in the republic of Croatia on 30 September 1978, 22 had been started in 1975 or earlier. As of the same date only 24.2 billion dinars' worth of work out of a total estimated value of 118.8 billion dinars on all 52 projects had been accomplished ('Prekoračenja . . .', 1978/9).

There is no bureaucratic reason why Yugoslav enterprises should overbid for investment resources in this way. Only a very small proportion of investment funds comes in the form of hand-outs, and enterprises have no need to fear any kind of confiscation of their assets. They are, in addition, free of any direct controls on how they allocate net income between accumulation and distributions. Certainly, getting a project started may help to put pressure on banks to extend credit (Banjanin, 1979). Certainly the combination of workers' self-management and local nationalism tends to foster a 'to each his own' pattern (Vlaho, 1979c). But as Branko Čolanović, the president of Jugobanka, has argued, it is the fact of negative real rates of interest, and the expectation of moratoria or other forms of bailing-out when projects run into trouble, that lie at the centre of the problem ('Zašto nema . . .', 1981). The Yugoslav interest structure was raised sharply in 1983, with the rate on term deposits with a term of more than three years rising to 28 per cent, and other rates going as high as 36 per cent. To put this into perspective, however, the rate of inflation of retail prices was 46 per cent in 1981. More fundamentally, the lack of clear responsibility for amortisation raises a question-mark over the whole price mechanism as it applies in the investment field ('Jedna mera . . .', 1983). The Yugoslav authorities have been at least as reluctant as the Hungarian to enforce socialist bankruptcy — for good socio-political reasons, given their unemployment problem — so that policies to reduce investment spread have in practice amounted to little more than freezes on investment finance which always allow so many exceptions that they cannot possibly be effective ('Na pomulu . . .', 1982) and weak planning agreements which do nothing to change the pattern of trade-offs as they appear to the enterprise ('Jedinstveno . . .', 1982). But we must repeat that there are no powerful pressures on Yugoslav managements to overbid for investment resources. In this case the mere *availability* of cheap investment funds seems to have been enough to create a serious problem of *raspylenie*.

Of course there must be countries round the world in which negative real rates of interest have not been accompanied by excessive investment spread on the East European pattern. We argued in Chapter 1 that *raspylenie* in the Soviet case is very much an aspect of the industry-based strategy for extensive growth. One of the most striking features of Yugoslav economic development over the last thirty years has been the extent to which the break with Soviet planning practice has *not* been accompanied by a break with Soviet development strategy. In Hungary the wholly inappropriate imposition of the same strategy was surely a major cause of the explosion in 1956. The shift from extensive to intensive development patterns in the investment sphere does, then, appear to involve very special difficulties, whether the extensive development strategy had actually been carried out successfully or not. On the one hand Hungarian and Yugoslav experience suggests that pragmatic middle ways will just not do in this sphere. On the other the most reform-minded of Soviet planners might be perplexed by the task of marketising something like the Baikal-Amur railway line project in the Soviet Far East. It is surely significant that design and R and D are two of the sectors singled out for possible free-contract treatment under the Bulgarian NEM. No doubt the Russians will be looking with particular interest at just how far the Bulgarians have to go to make substantial progress on the effectiveness of investment planning.

An element in Andropov's package of slogans which we have touched on only briefly up to now was highlighted in the late General Secretary's key article on the teaching of Karl Marx, published in early 1983.

The system functions and is perfected through the process of continually finding new forms and methods of developing democracy, extending the economic rights and opportunities of the working man on the production floor, and in all dimensions of socio-political activity . . . This is real socialist self-management of the people, which develops in the course of construction of full communism. (Andropov, 1983, p. 12)

Now the word we are translating as self-management is *samoupravlenie* – exactly the same word as the Serbo-Croat *samoupravljanje*, a term which has come to symbolise the Yugoslav system of semi-pluralistic market socialism. In the past the idea of self-management has been anathema to the Soviet leadership, and the Kremlin is certainly not looking for reformist inspiration from Yugoslav theory or practice, as has been made quite clear by Politburo member Aliev (Aliev, 1983). So what exactly does Andropov mean by 'real socialist self-management of the people'? A new law, 'On Working Collectives and How to Increase their Role in Management', has gone some way to giving the concept a concrete, operational content.

Yu. Tikhomirov, an Academy of Sciences jurist, sums up the spirit of the law in terms of a series of dialectical unities – the unity of rights and obligations, the unity of one-man management and participation, the unity of discipline and democracy (Tikhomirov, 1983). Another scholarly writer is more down to earth when he posits that 'working collectives . . . elaborate and adopt counterpart plans, confirm measures to raise labour productivity and socialist competition arrangements . . . apply social incentive measures . . . and impose penalties for infringements of labour discipline' (Samoshchenko, 1983). We have seen that socialist competitions and counterpart plans have in the Soviet Union been used largely as political instruments to make plans more taut, to counteract the tendency for managers and workers alike to seek a safety margin. If Soviet self-management is to mean nothing more than the enlistment of more shop-floor personnel in the campaign for extra-plan commimments (very much in the spirit of the 1979 planning decree) – coupled with the dubious privilege, for the erring worker, of being disciplined, formally at least, by his mates rather than the management – then it does not add up to very much.

But perhaps that is being too harsh, particularly if, under Bulgarian influence, the Soviet authorities begin to transform the nature of counterpart planning. As we saw in Chapter 4, Soviet agriculture is witnessing the introduction of schemes which involve genuine work-team autonomy in the administration of incentive funds. Certainly the Soviet leaders are primarily interested in the idea of self-management as a way of getting people to work harder. Certainly they would be justifiably sceptical about Yugoslav workers' councils' bad record on cost-inflationary pressures (Popov and Jovičić, 1971), and might find the kind of dog-fights between white- and blue-collar workers over wages and salaries that sometimes occur in the homeland of self-management rather appalling (see Dyker, 1983b, p. 13). But they would surely be very interested in the fact that the Kikinda foundry, in Vojvodina, has recently cut the working day to six hours, with a resultant increase in production and lowering in the incidence of sick-leave and accidents. In Belgrade 22 working organisations were preparing to introduce a shortened working day from 1 July 1983 ('Kraći radni dan', 1983). The general conclusion from Yugoslav experience is that with a shorter working day improved productivity comes from better organisation and more efficient use of work time, rather than any increase in the intensity of work. As we have seen in previous chapters, it is precisely organisation and efficient use of work time that have been the weakest points on the Soviet labour front. But the key question, of course, is whether hypothetical Soviet workers' councils could possibly effect such a painless intensification of the work process in the context of a planning system that had not undergone a radical transformation. Once again, then, we are back with the issue of general planning reform.

So what are the ultimate obstacles to decisive reform? Ideological conviction and sheer conservatism have induced important elements in the leadership to place more trust in the future of perfect computation than any sober prognostication could possibly warrant. We should not underestimate the strength of the notion, even among Soviet scholars and scientists, that there is no place for market forces in a socialist economy. But the fathers of the planning reform movement in the Soviet Union, all of them active in the formulation of the theory of optimal planning, were equally all agreed that the first condition of rationalisation of the planning system is substantial decentralisation. The saga of ineffectuality in the introduction of computers into Soviet planning in the 1970s testifies to the correctness of this proposition, as does much of the argument presented in this book. It is, then, difficult to impute the stiffening-up of the reform process to purely doctrinal and intellectual factors. To gain a fuller understanding we have to bring together some of the political strands we have picked up in earlier chapters.

Stalin abused the Communist Party as much as he did any other section of the Soviet society, though he did, of course, entrust to the Party professionals the vital trouble-shooting function without which no centrally planned system could possibly survive. Here is a snapshot of a day in the life of one of his apparatus men:

In the reception room of the deputy director for supply of the Kuznetsk Metallurgy Combine we happened to meet Comrade

Ivanov, an instructor in the heavy industry department of the Kemerovo Provincial Party Committee.

'As usual, I'm pushing things through,' explained Comrade Ivanov, as if justifying his presence here . . . In his briefcase lay a sheaf of letters and telegrams addressed to the Party committee from different departments. They were requests to push through or speed up an order for beams, for sheet steel, for steel structures, etc. . . . In the heavy industry department of the Kemerovo Party committee things are so organised that workers in the department frequently end up as intercessors — pushing through various kinds of *naryad* and other economic matters. When visiting enterprises, they call frequently on directors or head engineers, but scarcely throw a glance in the direction of the primary Party organisations. (Tarasov, 1950)

But it was only after the death of the dictator that the Party began to regularise its position as a stable privileged stratum within Soviet society, and as we saw in Chapter 3 the consolidation of Khrushchev's power, and the implementation of his early economic reforms, were intimately connected with the emergence of the regional Party apparatus as the dominant force in Soviet politics. It was precisely that force which, through its strength in the Central Committee of the Communist Party, was able to oust Khrushchev in 1964. The successor leadership of Brezhnev and Kosygin was a coalition of apparatus men and technocrats, but by the late 1960s it was clear that the apparatus element was, through the primacy of Brezhnev, to remain pre-eminent. It is easiest to document *apparatchik* resistance to specific autonomising experiments, like the agricultural link. Much more generally important is the proposition that the Communist Party apparatus had clearly perceived as early as 1968 how further decisive steps in the direction of general reform would unavoidably lead to a sharp diminution of their role in the process of continual adjustment whereby Soviet planning is made to work.

As we saw in Chapter 3, one of the factors facilitating that perception was observation of the way things had gone with a more radical approach to economic reform in Czechoslovakia in 1966–7. This immediately raises the issue of how the Hungarian Party apparatus could bring itself to swallow the radical marketising reform in 1968, or indeed how the Socialist Unity Party activists in East Germany have been persuaded to go along with reforms which, although low-key in formulation, have in practice brought much of the flexibility of a market economy back to East Germany. In fact, the very strength of purpose of Party/government strategy at the highest level in those countries has probably to a considerable extent been conditioned by the weakness of the parties as socio-political organisations. The Hungarian Party had to be rebuilt from scratch after the revolution of 1956, while Kadar, Hungarian supremo from 1956 to the present day, was in any case embarking on his preliminary round of planning reforms as early as 1957. Thus the Hungarian Party apparatus never had the opportunity to build up a strong vested interest in the traditional planning system which had, in any case, been particularly ineffectual in Hungary. In East Germany the Party has never, for reasons which hardly need rehearsing, had much standing amongst the population at large, while the instruments of political control in East Germany are still to a substantial extent in the hands of the Soviet military and police (Myagkov, 1976). In both these countries, then, a genuinely equal partnership with the technocracy may have seemed the best of all possible alternatives to the apparatus man, the more so that the quality of East German and Hungarian technocracy is high by Eastern European standards. To the extent that the very success of the traditional Soviet planning system in fostering growth in its country of origin has consolidated the position of the apparatus, it has made the process of redirecting the planning system that much more difficult.

The recent changes in the leadership have certainly signalled no dramatic change in the balance of political power within the Soviet Union. The Party apparatus remains supreme, but the specifically military and police interests have come more into the forefront, as indeed they were beginning to do during the late Brezhnev period. Does this make any difference to the prospects for economic reform? The predominant view is that quality control has not been a problem in the Soviet defence industry in the way it has in Soviet industry as a whole (Campbell, 1972), and that weapons systems have on the whole been comparable in effectiveness to corresponding Western systems (Checinski, 1981). Certainly this picture fits in with our argument that Soviet-type planning systems can be very good at doing a limited number of very specific things. On the other hand Soviet backwardness in computer hardware must surely affect the *overall* effectiveness of Soviet defence, and the Korean airliner tragedy suggests strongly that communications systems are not all that they might be. Andropov made some remarks in late 1983 which suggest that he believed that the United States is building up a lead over the Russians in nuclear military technology (BBC, 1983). Of course the remarks may have been made with world public opinion very much in mind, but Western press reports suggest that Chernenko shared Andropov's fears (Owen, 1984). On balance we must conclude that Soviet military leaders, and indeed Party and government leaders, when considering defence matters, must see some value for the effectiveness of the defence effort in the more radical planning reform proposals.

Once again, however, the crucial question is the trade-off between quality and quantity. There is currently a disagreement between the CIA and the Defense Intelligence Agency in the United States about the trend in Soviet defence spending in ruble terms as a proportion of national income. The CIA's calculations indicate that the proportion has been steady at 12-14 per cent since 1970. The DIA reckons that it has risen from 13-14 per cent in 1970 to 14-16 per cent in 1981 (Joint Economic Committee, US Congress, 1983). Of course the margin of error in these estimates, which aim to correct by intelligence means the grossly misleading official Soviet military budget figures, must be large. What we can conclude safely is that the Soviet Union continues in a period of sharply falling growth rates to devote what is by international standards an unusually high proportion of national income to defence. However much the priority principle may have weakened within the civilian economy, there can be no doubt that it still operates powerfully in favour of defence. The Soviet military leadership must see this as one good reason for sticking to the command economy, since surely only the command economy can guarantee absolute priority. At the same time the Soviet leadership as a whole must be a little concerned that the combination of defence ratios around 15 per cent and investment ratios around 30 per cent leaves little more than half of national income for communal and private consumption purposes. Consumption of goods in the Soviet Union was still growing by 2.1 per cent per annum in the period 1976-80, according to the CIA (Schroeder and Denton, 1982, p. 326), but if overall growth rates continue to fall, then continuation of the somewhat faltering upward trend in consumption might be called into question. If we believe that it is politically essential for the Soviet leadership to ensure that consumption does keep on growing, then we could imagine a scenario where the maintenance of defence votes might present an increasingly strong argument in favour of radical economic reform

(1) as a general basis for raising overall growth rates;
(2) more specifically as a means of increasing investment effectiveness, which would make it possible either to grow faster, or to

reduce the investment ratio, or a bit of both.

The big stumbling-block on the reform road as far as the military are concerned would, of course, be the problem of transition. We have argued that the kind of radical planning reform the Soviet economy really needs would probably involve a fairly extended and painful transitional period, as the economy was reorganised and restructured, as uneconomic capacities were liquidated and surplus workers re-deployed. In the short run growth rates would certainly go down rather than up, though qualitative improvements might have a substantial and rapid positive effect on the balance of payments. Party and military interests, then, are likely to combine to ensure a continuation of the attempt to substitute piecemeal rationalisation for thoroughgoing reform. But there *are* organisational and technological imperatives, or at least conditions for long-term survival. With the Western econo-mies picking up again, the pressures on the Soviet government to do something decisive to improve the quantitative and qualitative performance of the economy can only grow stronger.

GLOSSARY

apparatchik	Communist Party apparatus man
CMEA	Council for Mutual Economic Assistance
CRE	coefficient of relative effectiveness
ekspertiza	design monitoring organisation
gektarshchik	'hectarer'
glavk	main administration (within ministry)
Gosbank	State Bank
Goskomtrud	All-Union State Committee for Labour and Social Problems
Gosplan	State Planning Commission
Gossnab	State Supply Committee
Gosstroi	State Construction Committee
khozraschet	'business accounting'
kolkhoz	collective farm
kolkhoznik	collective farmer
Komsomol	Young Communist League
kontrol'nye tsifry	'control figures'
krai	province
KTU (*koeffitsient trudovogo uchastiya*)	labour coefficient
Minstroi	Ministry of Construction
naryad	allocation certificate
NMP	net material product (Marxian definition of national income which excludes 'unproductive services')
NNO	normed net output
ob"edinenie	association
oblast'	province
Orgnabor	organised recruitment
PBR	payment by results
PCIA	production construction and installation association

planirovanie ot dostignutogo urovnya	'planning from the achieved level'
Politburo	Political Bureau, Communist Party Cabinet
proektnaya organizatsiya	design organisation
propiska	residence permit
RAPO (*raionnoe agro-promyshlennoe ob"edinenie*)	district agro-industrial association
raspylenie (sredstv)	excessive investment spread
Sel'khozkhimiya	chemicals for agriculture organisation
Sel'khoztekhnika	machinery for agriculture organisation
shturmovshchina	'storming'
snabsbyt	supply depot
sovkhoz	state farm
sovnarkhoz	Regional Economic Council
Stroibank	Investment Bank
tekuchest'	excessive labour turnover
TEOs (*tekhniko-ekonomicheskie obosnovaniya*)	feasibility studies
titul'nyi spisok	'title list'
tolkach	'pusher'
trudoustroistvo	labour placement
upravlenie	administration
val, valovaya produktsiya	gross output
vstrechnye plany	'counterpart plans'
yarmarki	wholesale fairs
zayavka	indent, requisition
zveno	link

REFERENCES

Abalkin, L. (1977) 'Upravlenie i ego rezervy', *Pravda*, 27 May, p. 3

Abouchar, A. (1967) 'Rationality in the prewar Soviet cement industry', *Soviet Studies, 19* (2)

Adam, J. (1980) 'The present Soviet incentive system', *Soviet Studies, 32* (3)

'A esli vniknut'' (1968) *Pravda*, 15 November, p. 2

Agaev, E. (1981) 'Personal'nyi gektar', *Literaturnaya Gazeta*, 18 March, p. 10

Aksenov, K. (1980) 'Dat' prostor novomu', *Pravda*, 26 October, p. 2

Aliev, G. (1983) Speech on the draft law on working collectives, *Pravda*, 18 June, p. 2

Aliev, N. (1980) 'Proigryvaet . . . peredovik', *Pravda*, 20 September, p. 2

Amann, R., Cooper, J. and Davis, R.W. (eds.) (1977) *The Technological Level of Soviet Industry*, Yale University Press, New Haven and London

Andriyanov, V. (1971) 'Problemy kadrov dal'nego vostoka; 2. pereselenets', *Komsomol'skaya Pravda*, 24 July, p. 2

Andropov, Yu. (1982) Speech reported in *Pravda*, 23 November

—— (1983) 'Uchenie Karla Marksa i nekotorye voprosy sotsialisticheskogo stroitel'stva v SSSR', *Voprosy Ekonomiki* (3)

Aparin, N.P. (1983) 'O rasprostranenii shchekinskogo metoda uvelicheniya ob''emov priozvodstva s men'shei chislennost'yu', *Ekonomicheskaya Gazeta* (49), 6

Bakhtaryshev, Sh. (1980) 'Organizatsiya i oplate truda zhivotnovodov', *Ekonomicheskaya Gazeta* (43), 19

Banjanin, N. (1979) 'Prekomjerna investicijska potrošnja', *Privredni Vjesnik*, 19 November, p. 7

Barsukov, I. V. (1971) 'Effektivnost' podsobnogo promysla', *Sel'skoe Khozyaistvo Belorussii* (7)

BBC (1983) *Summary of World Broadcasts*, SU/7452/A1, 30 September

Bergson, A. (1964) *The Economics of Soviet Planning*, Yale University Press, New Haven

—— (1978) *Productivity and the Social System – the USSR and the West*, Harvard University Press, Cambridge, Mass.

Berliner, J. (1966) 'Managerial incentives and decision-making: a comparison of the United States and the Soviet Union' in M. Bornstein and D.R. Fusfeld (eds.), *The Soviet Economy – a Book of Readings*, 2nd edn, Irwin, Homewood, Ill.

Bezdelev, V. (1983) 'Zarplata i proizvoditel'nost'', *Ekonomicheskaya Gazeta* (42), 18

Birman, I. (1978) '"From the achieved level"', *Soviet Studies, 30* (2)

Bodashevskii, I. (1968) 'Dva predlozheniya', *Ekonomicheskaya Gazeta* (16), 10

Bogomolov, F. (1982) 'I stala niva shchedree', *Ekonomicheskaya Gazeta* (8), 14

Boldyrev, A. (1979) 'Planirovanie v otrasli – na novuyu stupen'', *Ekonomicheskaya Gazeta* (48), 7

Boot, P. (1983) 'Continuity and change in the planning system of the German Democratic Republic', *Soviet Studies, 35* (3)

Brezhnev, L. I. (1982) 'O Prodovol'stvennoi Programme SSSR na period do 1990 goda i merakh po ee realizatsii', *Ekonomischeskaya Gazeta* (22)

Bronshtein, D. F. (1970) 'Kompleks kak uchetnaya edinitsa v promyshlennom

stroitel'stve i faktor, sposobstvuyushchii sokrashcheniyu ob"ema nezaver-
shennogo stroitel'stva' in *Metody i Praktika Opredeleniya Effektivnosti
Kapital'nykh Vlozhenii i Novoi Tekhniki*, issue 17, Nauka, Moscow

Bulgakov, S. (1983) 'Nachinaetsya s plana', *Pravda*, 7 September, p. 2

Bullock, A. and Stallybrass, O. (eds.) (1977) *The Fontana Dictionary of Modern Thought*, Collins, London

Bunich, P. (1967) 'Khozyaistvennaya reforma v promyshlennosti: ee osushchestv-lenie i nekotorye problemy', *Voprosy Ekonomiki* (10)

Campbell, R. W. (1972) 'Management spillovers from Soviet space and military programmes', *Soviet Studies, 23* (4)

Cave, M. (1980) *Computers and Economic Planning: the Soviet Experience*, Cambridge University Press, Cambridge

—— and Hare, P. (1981) *Alternative Approaches to Economic Planning*, Macmillan, London

Checinski, M. (1981) *The Military-Industrial Complex in the USSR*, No. AZ 2303, Stiftung Wissenschaft und Politik, Ebenhausen, September

Chenery, H. and Watanabe, T. (1958) 'International comparisons of the structure of production', *Econometrica, 26* (4)

Chernyavskii, L. (1976) 'Stroikam − snabzhenie po zakazam', *Ekonomicheskaya Gazeta* (6), 10

Clark, H. Gardner (1956) *The Economics of Soviet Steel*, Harvard University Press, London

Clarke, R. A. and Matko, D. J. I. (1983) *Soviet Economic Facts 1917–81*, Macmillan, London

Conquest, R. (1968) *The Great Terror*, Macmillan, London

Conyngham, W. (1982) *The Modernization of Soviet Industrial Management*, Cambridge University Press, Cambridge

Cooper, J. (1979) *Innovation for Innovation in Soviet Industry*, Centre for Russian and East European Studies discussion paper, University of Birmingham, June

Csikos-Nagy, B. (1978) 'The Hungarian reform after ten years', *Soviet Studies, 30* (4)

Demchenko, V. (1965) 'Ne opekat'!', *Ekonomicheskaya Gazeta*, 13 October, p. 6

Dementsev, V. V. (1975) 'Finansovyi mekhanizm ob"edinenii', *Ekonomicheskaya Gazeta* (25), 8

Devons, E. (1950) *Planning in Practice*, Cambridge University Press, Cambridge

Dorfman, R., Samuelson, P. and Solow, R. (1958) *Linear Programming and Economic Analysis*, McGraw-Hill, New York

Drogichinskii, N. (1974) 'Ob optovoi torgovli sredstvami proizvodstva', *Voprosy Ekonomiki* (4)

Dudorov, N. (1982) 'Kakov urozhai − takova i oplata', *Ekonomicheskaya Gazeta* (22), 18

—— (1983) 'Zainteresovannost' v konechnykh rezul'tatakh', *Ekonomicheskaya Gazeta* (33), 15

—— and Kozlov, E. (1984) 'Chabany rabotayut na podryade', *Ekonomicheskaya Gazeta* (12), 17

Dyker, D. A. (1976) *The Soviet Economy*, Crosby Lockwood Staples, London

—— (1981a) 'Planning and the worker' in L. Schapiro and J. Godson (eds.), *The Soviet Worker*, Macmillan, London

—— (1981b) 'Decentralisation and the command principle − some lessons from Soviet experience', *Journal of Comparative Economics, 5* (2)

—— (1983a) *The Process of Investment in the Soviet Union*, Cambridge University Press, Cambridge

—— (1983b) 'The crisis in Yugoslav self-management', *Contemporary Review, 242* (January)

—— (1984) 'The economy' in D. R. Jones (ed.), *Soviet Armed Forces Review Annual*, vol. 7, Academic International Press, Gulf Breeze, Fl.

Economic Commission for Europe (1977a) *Economic Bulletin for Europe, 29*, United Nations, New York

Economic Commission for Europe (1977b) *Economic Survey of Europe in 1976*, Part I, United Nations, New York

Economic Commission for Europe (1978) *Economic Survey of Europe in 1977*, United Nations, New York

Economic Commission for Europe (1980) *Economic Bulletin for Europe, 31* (2), United Nations, New York

Economic Commission for Europe (1982) *Economic Survey of Europe in 1981*, United Nations, New York

Economic Commission for Europe (1983) *Economic Survey of Europe in 1982*, United Nations, New York

Economic Commission for Europe (1984) *Economic Survey of Europe in 1983*, United Nations, New York

Efimov, A. N. (1957) *Perestroika Upravleniya Promyshlennost'yu i Stroitel'stvom v SSSR*, Gospolizdat, Moscow

Ekonomicheskie Problemy Agrarno-promyshlennoi Integratsii (1976) Kolos, Moscow

Ellman, M. (1970) 'The consistency of Soviet plans' in M. Bornstein and D. R. Fusfeld (eds.), *The Soviet Economy – a Book of Readings*, 3rd edn, Irwin, Homewood, Ill.

—— (1979) *Socialist Planning*, Cambridge University Press, Cambridge

Emchenko, F. (1983) 'Podryad na molochnom komplekse', *Ekonomicheskaya Gazeta* (39), 15

Engels, F. (1962) *Anti-Dühring*, 3rd edn, Foreign Languages Publishing House, Moscow

Erlich, A. (1960) *The Soviet Industrialisation Debate*, Harvard University Press, Cambridge, Mass.

Fedorenko, K. G. and Yandovskii, G. V. (1976) 'Kapitalovlozheniya i kontrol' Stroibanka', *Finansy SSSR* (2)

Fedorenko, N. (1968) 'Ob ekonomicheskoi otsenke prirodnykh resursov', *Voprosy Ekonomiki* (3)

Ferberg, A. (1966) 'O kapital'nykh vlozheniyakh na rekonstruktsiyu deistvuyush-chikh predpriyatii', *Voprosy Ekonomiki* (1)

Fil'ev, V. (1983) 'Shchekinskii metod i perspektivy ego dal'neishego razvitiya', *Voprosy Ekonomiki* (2)

Filippov, P. (1983) 'V chem sila gektara', *Ekonomicheskaya Gazeta* (24), 13

Food and Agriculture Organization (1982) *FAO Trade Yearbook 1981*, vol. 35, Rome

—— (1983) *FAO Trade Yearbook 1982*, vol. 36, Rome

Fridenberg, V. (1957) 'Voprosy kombinirovaniya proizvodstva', *Voprosy Ekonomiki* (9)

Galkin, D. (1976) 'Povysit' effektivnost' rekonstruktsii', *Ekonomicheskaya Gazeta* (1), 7

Gerschenkron, A. (1966) *Economic Backwardness in Historical Perspective*, Harvard University Press, Cambridge, Mass.

Gillula, J. W. and Bond, D. L. (1977) 'Development of regional Input-Output analysis in the Soviet Union' in V. G. Treml (ed.), *Studies in Soviet Input-Output Analysis*, Praeger, New York and London

Gladyshev, A. (1966) 'Obshchestvennye fondy potrebleniya i migratsiya naseleniya', *Planovoe Khozyaistvo* (10)

Gofman, K. and Petrakov, N. (1968) 'Tsenoobrazovanie s pozitsii tekhnicheskogo progressa', *Ekonomicheskaya Gazeta* (27), 11

Golub', E. (1974) 'Bol'shoi konveier', *Pravda*, 13 May, p. 1

Gomanov, V. (1981) 'Kolkhozu podspor'e', *Pravda*, 29 April, p. 3

Goncharov, I. (1984) 'Sebestoimost' − pokazatel' opredelyayushchii', *Ekonomicheskaya Gazeta* (10), 8

Gorushkin, V. (1969) 'Za schet fonda razvitiya . . .', *Ekonomicheskaya Gazeta* (15), 6

Granick, D. (1980) 'The ministry as the maximising unit in Soviet industry', *Journal of Comparative Economics, 4* (3)

Gray, K. R. (1979) 'Soviet agricultural specialisation and efficiency', *Soviet Studies, 31* (4)

Green, D. W. (1984) Review of D. A. Dyker, *The Process of Investment in the Soviet Union, Soviet Studies, 36* (2)

Greenslade, R. (1976) 'The real National Product of the USSR 1950-75' in Joint Economic Committee, US Congress, *Soviet Economy in a New Perspective*, USGPO, Washington, DC

Gregory, P. and Stuart, R. (1981) *Soviet Economic Structure and Performance*, 2nd edn, Harper and Row, New York

Gribov, V. (1976) 'Sovershenstvovanie planirovaniya i finansirovaniya kapital'nykh vlozhenii', *Planovoe Khozyaistvo* (7)

Gusev, N. (1970) 'Sel'skoe khozyaistvo v zavershayushchem godu pyatiletki', *Ekonomika Sel'skogo Khozyaistva* (3)

—— (1971) 'Sel'skoe khozyaistvo v pervom godu novoi pyatiletki', *Ekonomika Sel'skogo Khozyaistva* (2)

Hanson, P. (1968) *The Consumer Sector in the Soviet Economy*, Northwestern University Press, Evanston, Ill.

—— (1983) 'Success indicators revisited: the July 1979 Soviet decree on planning and management', *Soviet Studies, 35* (1)

—— (1984) 'Brezhnev's economic legacy' in *NATO Colloquium 1984*, NATO Economics and Information Directorates, Brussels

—— and Hill, R. M. (1979) 'Soviet assimilation of western technology; a survey of UK exporters' experience' in Joint Economic Committee, US Congress, *Soviet Economy in a Time of Change*, USGPO, Washington, DC

Hare, P. (1979) 'Investment in Hungary: the planners' nightmare', paper presented at the National Association for Soviet and East European Studies annual conference, 24-26 March, held at Fitzwilliam College, Cambridge

—— (1983) 'The beginnings of institutional reform in Hungary', *Soviet Studies, 35* (3)

Heal, G. (1973) *The Theory of Economic Planning*, North Holland Publishing House, Amsterdam and Oxford

Hirschman, A. (1958) *The Strategy of Economic Development*, Yale University Press, New Haven

Holzman, F. (1957) 'The Soviet Urals-Kuznetsk combine', *Quarterly Journal of Economics, 71* (3)

Hunter, H. (1964) 'Priorities and shortfalls in pre-war Soviet planning' in J. Degras and A. Nove (eds.), *Soviet Planning. Essays in Honour of Naum Jasny*, Blackwell, Oxford

Hutchings, R. (1976) *Soviet Science, Technology, Design*, Oxford University Press, London

Isaev, V. (1973) 'Puti povysheniya effektivnosti kapital'nykh vlozhenii', *Voprosy Ekonomiki* (8)

Iskinderov, I. (1983) 'Bez vedomstvennykh bar'erov', *Ekonomicheskaya Gazeta* (35), 13

Ivanov, L. (1968) 'Na tekh li dorogakh ishchem?', *Literaturnaya Gazeta*, 25 September, p. 10

Ivanov, V. (1979) Statement in *Ekonomicheskaya Gazeta* (21), 9

Jasny, N. (1972) *Soviet Economists of the Twenties: Names to be Remembered*, Cambridge University Press, Cambridge

'Jedinstveno o investicijama' (1982) *Ekonomska Politika*, 15 November, p. 11

'Jedna mera – mnogo efekata' (1983) *Ekonomska Politika*, 17 January, p. 5

Joint Economic Committee, US Congress (1982) *USSR: Measures of Economic Growth and Development, 1950-80*, USGPO, Washington, DC

—— (1983) 'Soviet Defense Trends', September

Kalmykov, G. and Filipenko, V. (1966) 'Zolotoe dno', *Don* (10)

Kantorovich, L. (1939) *Mathematicheskie Metody Organizatsii i Planirovaniya Proizvodstva*, Leningrad University Press, Leningrad

—— and Vainshtein, A. (1967) 'Ob ischislenii normy effektivnosti na osnove odnoproduktovoi modeli razvitiya narodnogo khozyaistva', *Ekonomika i Mathematicheskie Metody* (5)

——, —— (1970) 'Eschche ob ischislenii normy effektivnosti na osnove odnoproduktovoi modeli razvitiya narodnogo khozyaistva', *Ekonomika i Mathematicheskie Metody* (3)

Karcz, J. F. (1968) 'Soviet agriculture: a balance sheet' in V. G. Treml (ed.), *The Development of the Soviet Economy: Plan and Performance*, Praeger, New York

Kaser, M. (1975) 'The economy: a general assessment' in A. Brown and M. Kaser (eds.), *The Soviet Union since the Fall of Khrushchev*, Macmillan, London

Katsenelinboigen, A. (1978) *Studies in Soviet Economic Planning*, M. E. Sharpe, White Plains, NY

Keren, M. (1972) 'On the tautness of plans', *Review of Economic Studies, 39* (4)

Khashkin, G. Z. *et al.* (1975) *Osnovnye Fondy Gazovoi Promyshlennosti*, Nedra, Moscow

Khashutogov, V. (1976) 'Kogda narushaetsya distsiplina postavok', *Ekonomicheskaya Gazeta* (37), 10

Khikmatov, A. (1969) *Reservy Povysheniya Effektivnosti Kapital'nykh Vlozhenii*, Uzbekistan, Tashkent

Kirillov, N. (1975) 'Kazhdoi stroike – ekonomichnyi proekt', *Ekonomicheskaya Gazeta* (47), 9

Kirov, Kh. (1983) 'O novom ekonomiescheskom mekhanizme v NRB', *Voprosy Ekonomiki* (5)

Knyazev, Yu. (1983) 'Uchastie trudyashchikhsya v upravlenii proizvodstvom v evropeiskikh stranakh SEV', *Voprosy Ekonomiki* (6)

Kolesnevov, S. G. (1971) 'Ekonomicheskoe stimulirovanie i oplata truda v sel'skom khozyaistve' in V. F. Mel'nikov (ed.), *Ekonomika Sotsialisticheskogo Sel'skogo Khozyaistva v Sovremennykh Usloviyakh*, Ekonomika, Moscow

'Kollektivnyi podryad na sele' (1983) *Ekonomicheskaya Gazeta* (30), 11

Komarov, I. (1979) 'Zarplata stroitelya', *Ekonomicheskaya Gazeta* (12), 9

Konovalova, T. (1983) 'Otvetstvennost' za pole', *Ekonomicheskaya Gazeta* (31), 18

Koppel', F. and Brig, B. (1969) 'Bol'shoi gorod i ministerstva', *Pravda*, 21 May, p. 2

Koprivica, V. (1979) 'Težak teret dugova', *Privredni Vjesnik*, 17 December, p. 5

Kopteva, A. (1983) 'Khozyaeva polya', *Ekonomicheskaya Gazeta* (36), 16

Kopysov, I. (1968) 'Krestyanin i zemlya', *Literaturnaya Gazeta* (6), 10

Kornai, J. (1969) 'Multi-level programming – a first report on the model and on the experimental computations', *European Economic Review, 1* (1)

Kozlov, N. (1982) 'Kollektivnaya otvetstvennost' za urozhai', *Ekonomicheskaya Gazeta* (26), 7

'Kraći radni dan' (1983) *Ekonomska Politika*, 31 January, p. 7

Kritsman, L. (1921) *O Edinom Khozyaistvennom Plane*, Gosizdat, Moscow

Kudashov, E. (1983) 'Most mezhdu starym i novym', *Ekonomika Stroitel'stva* (9)

Kudryadtsev, V. *et al.* (1968) 'Ekonomicheskie etalony i konkursnoe proektirovanie', *Ekonomika Stroitel'stva* (3)

Kulagin, G. (1982) 'Trudno byt' universalom', *Pravda*, 8 December, p. 2

Kulenis, A. (1984) 'Vysokoe kachestvo obuslovleno dogovorom', *Ekonomicheskaya Gazeta* (13) 6

Kuz'mich, Yu. A. (1983) 'Neobkhodimye predplanovye proektnye prorabotki – put' k povysheniyu effektivnosti kapital'nykh vlozhenii', *Ekonomika Stroitel'stva* (9)

Lavelle, M. J. (1974) 'The Soviet "New Method" pricing formulae', *Soviet Studies, 26* (1)

Lenin, V. I. (1966) 'Ob edinom khozyaistvennom plane' in *Izbrannye Proizvedeniya*, Political Literature Publishing House, Moscow, vol. 3

Leontief, W. (1936) 'Quantitative Input/Output relations in the economic system of the United States', *Review of Economics and Statistics, 18* (3)

Liberman, E. (1962) 'Plan, pribyl', premii', *Pravda*, 9 September, p. 3

Liberman, Ya. (1968) 'Ekonomicheskaya reforma i finansovoe planirovanie', *Planovoe Khozyaistvo* (3)

Lifatov, A. P. (1980) 'Uporyadochit' obespechenie stroek nerudnymi materialami', *Ekonomika Stroitel'stva* (4)

Logach, N. (1983) 'Soglasovyat' plany i deistviya', *Ekonomicheskaya Gazeta* (24), 12

Lupton, T. (1972) 'On the shop floor: output and earnings' in T. Lupton (ed.), *Payments Systems*, Penguin, Harmondsworth

Lur'e, S. (1973) 'Dogovor na izgotovlenie i realizatsiyu produktsii podsobnykh prepriyatii i promyslov sel'skogo khozyaistva', *Sotsialisticheskoe Zakonodatel'stvo* (1)

Marx, K. (1968) 'Critique of the Gotha Programme' in K. Marx and F. Engels, *Selected Works*, Lawrence and Wishart, London

Matthews, M. (1978) *Privilege in the Soviet Union*, George Allen and Unwin, London

Melzer, M. (1981) 'Combine formation in the GDR', *Soviet Studies, 33* (1)

Metodika Opredeleniya Ekonomicheskoi Effektivnosti Kapital'nykh Vlozhenii (1981), *Ekonomicheskaya Gazeta* (2 and 3)

Mirgaleev, A. (1977) 'Shchekinskii metod i ego perspektivy', *Voprosy Ekonomiki* (10)

Mironov, V. (1983) 'Komu vesti predproektyne raboty?', *Ekonomicheskaya Gazeta* (39), 19

Mitrofanov, A. (1969) 'Kompas ekonomicheskoi effektivnosti', *Ekonomicheskaya Gazeta* (39), 13

Monogarov, E. (1980) 'Fermy u terrikonov', *Pravda*, 13 November, p. 3

Mukhtarov, Kh. (1983) 'Mera truda – urozhai', *Ekonomicheskaya Gazeta* (26), 12–13

Myagkov, A. (1976) *Inside the KGB*, Foreign Affairs Publishing, Richmond, Va.

'Na pomolu organičenje?' (1982) *Ekonomska Politika*, 28 June, p. 12

Nasyrov, F. G. (1983) 'Rezul'taty analiziruem ezhemesechno', *Ekonomicheskaya Gazeta* (23), 13

National Board for Prices and Incomes (1968) Report No. 65, *Payment by Results Systems*, Cmnd. 3627, HMSO, London

National Bureau of Economic Research (1974) 54th Annual Report, *Issues for Research*, September

Nove, A. (1961) *The Soviet Economy*, George Allen and Unwin, London

—— (1968) *The Soviet Economy*, 3rd edn, George Allen and Unwin, London
—— (1969) *An Economic History of the USSR*, Allen Lane The Penguin Press, Harmondsworth
Oblomskaya, I., Strakhov, A. and Umanets, L. (1983) 'Sotsial'no-ekonomicheskaya odnorodnost' truda', *Voprosy Ekonomiki* (6)
'Ob uluchshenii planirovaniya i ekonomicheskogo stimulirovaniya proizvodstva i zagotovok sel'skokhozyaistvennykh produktov' (1980) *Ekonomicheskaya Gazeta* (52), 5–7
'Ob uluchshenii planirovaniya i usilenii vozdeistviya khozyaistvennogo mekhanizma na povyshenie effektivnosti proizvodstva i kachestva raboty' (1979) *Ekonomicheskaya Gazeta* (32), special supplement
'O dal'neishem ukreplenii trudovoi distsipliny i sokrashchenii tekuchesti kadrov v narodnom khozyaistve' (1980) *Ekonomicheskaya Gazeta* (3), 4
Otsason, R. (1983) 'Upravlenie sel'skokhozyaistvennymi predpriyatiyami v Vengrii', *Voprosy Ekonomiki* (1)
Ovdienko, M. (1984) 'Eksperiment i ucheba kadrov', *Ekonomicheskaya Gazeta* (7), 12
Owen, R. (1984) 'Ustinov in early-strike threat to Washington', *The Times*, 21 May, p. 1
Pavitt, K. (ed.) (1980) *Technical Innovation and British Economic Performance*, Macmillan, London
Pavlov, D. (1983) 'Agrotsekhi kooperatorov', *Ekonomicheskaya Gazeta* (35), 13
Perepechin, I. and Apraksina, L. (1980) 'Kakov proekt – takov ob"ekt', *Ekonomicheskaya Gazeta* (6), 7
Pessel', M. (1977) 'Kredit kak faktor intensifikatsii kapital'nogo stroitel'stva', *Planovoe Khozyaistvo* (1), 51
Petrasinović, P. (1980) 'Karakteristike ciklusa 1976-80', *Ekonomska Politika*, 1 September, pp. 22–6
Petrov, G. (1982) 'Na osnove kollektivnogo podryada', *Ekonomicheskaya Gazeta* (25), 7
Pilipas, V. and Polozenko, D. (1983) 'Kredit i khozraschet v kolkhozakh', *Ekonomicheskaya Gazeta* (30), 15
Plan Fulfilment Report for 1983 (1984) *Ekonomicheskaya Gazeta* (6), 7–9
'Planovye pokazateli kriterii otsenki' (1979) *Ekonomicheskaya Gazeta* (35), 5
Platoshkin, A. and Utkin, N. (1983) 'Vsemi zven'yami kompleksa', *Pravda*, 28 November, p. 2
Plyatsuk, V. and Andrusenko, Yu. (1984) 'Tseli novye, a metody starye . . .', *Ekonomicheskaya Gazeta* (10), 8
Podshivalenko, P. (ed.) (1965) *Ekonomika Stroitel'stva*, Political Literature Publishing House, Moscow
—— (1983) 'Organizatsionnye formy stroitel'stva i upravleniya im', *Voprosy Ekonomiki* (7)
—— and Evstigneev, V. D. (1980) 'Puti sovershenstvovaniya stroitel'nogo proizvodstva', *Ekonomika Stroitel'stva* (5)
Poltoranin, M. and Sevest'yanov, V. (1977) 'Na beregakh Irtysha', *Pravda*, 3 July, p. 2
Popov, S. and Jovičić, M. (1971) *Uticaj Licnih Dohodaka na Kretanje Cena*, Institut Ekonomskih Nauka, Belgrade
'Poryadok raspredeleniya pribyli' (1979) *Ekonomicheskaya Gazeta* (47), 10
Pospielovsky, D. (1970) 'The "link system" in Soviet agriculture', *Soviet Studies*, 21 (4)
Pozdnyakov, V. (1968) 'Razmeshchenie i razvitie podsobnoi promyshlennosti v kolkhozakh', *Ekonomika Sel'skogo Khozyaistva* (5)

'Prekoračenja u Hrvatskoj' (1978/9) *Privredni Vjesnik*, 30 December/9 January, p. 3

Primakov, A. (1983) 'S men'shim chislom rabotayushchikh', *Ekonomicheskaya Gazeta* (33), 14

'Problemy razrabotki novoi metodiki sostavleniya narodnokhozyaistvennykh planov' (1977) *Planovoe Khozyaistvo* (7)

Prodovol'stvennaya Programma SSSR na period do 1990 goda (1982) *Ekonomicheskaya Gazeta* (23), special supplement

Pronin, A. (1969) 'Razvitie podsobnykh predpriyatii i promyslov v kolkhozakh i sovkhozakh', *Ekonomika Sel'skogo Khozyaistva* (4)

Protsenko, O. D. and Soloveichik, D. I. (1976) *Planirovanie Dolgovremmenykh Khozyaistvennykh Svyazei*, Ekonomika, Moscow

Rabinovich, I. A. (1976) *Organizatsiya Snabzheniya i Effektivnost' Proizvodstva*, Tekhnika, Kiev

Radio Svoboda (1982) 'Materialy issledovatel'skogo otdela', RS 21/82, 5 February

Research on Soviet and East European Agriculture (1983), *5* (2)

Revenok, L. and Pichugin, P. (1981) 'Kogda poryadok na zemle', *Ekonomicheskaya Gazeta* (5), 19

'Rezervy agrarnoi ekonomiki' (1984) *Ekonomicheskaya Gazeta* (14), 3–5

Reznik, S. D. (1980) 'Trudovaya distsiplina', *Ekonomika Stroitel'stva* (3)

Rogin, S. (1979) 'Ispitany', *Pravda*, 9 October, p. 2

Roy, D. (1972) 'Quota restriction and goldbricking in a machine shop' in T. Lupton (ed.), *Payment Systems*, Penguin, Harmondsworth

Rumer, B. (1981) 'The "second" agriculture in the USSR', *Soviet Studies, 33* (4)

Ryzhov, M. (1972) 'Posylayut "tolkachei" . . . kogda podvodyat partnery', *Pravda*, 25 February, p. 3

Sadykov, V. (1983) 'Po-khozyaiski, s vysokoi otdachei', *Ekonomicheskaya Gazeta* (45), 16

Samoshchenko, I. (1983) 'Kollektiv v sisteme upravleniya', *Ekonomicheskaya Gazeta* (35), 10

Sushkin, Yu. G., Nikol'skii, I. V. and Korovitsyn, V. P. (eds.) (1967) *Ekonomicheskaya Geografiya SSSR*, Part I, Moscow University Press, Moscow

Schroeder, G. (1968) 'Soviet economic "reforms": a study in contradictions', *Soviet Studies, 20* (1)

——— and Denton, M. E. (1982) 'An index of consumption in the USSR' in Joint Economic Committee, US Congress (1982)

——— and Severin, B. (1976) 'Soviet consumption and income in perspective' in Joint Economic Committee, US Congress, *Soviet Economy in a New Perspective*, USGPO, Washington, DC

Schwarz, S. (1953) *Labour in the Soviet Union*, Cresset Press, London

Semenov, V. (1983) 'Effektivnost' raboty NPO', *Ekonomicheskaya Gazeta* (30), 9

Sergienkov, I. (1976) 'Kak griby posle dozhdya', *Pravda*, 8 May, p. 2

Shatunovskii, I. (1968) Report published in *Pravda*, 19 December, p. 2

Shavlyuk, V. (1979) 'Pochemu dorozhaet stroika', *Pravda*, 27 June, p. 2

Shirobokov, S. (1980) 'Inzhener ili ekspeditor', *Pravda*, 16 June, p. 2

Shiryaev, G. (1977) 'Uluchshenie proektno-smetnogo dela – vazhnaya narodno-khozyaistvennaya zadacha', *Planovoe Khozyaistvo* (1)

Shmelev, I. (1981) 'Obshchestvennoe proizvodstvo i lichnoe podsobnoe khozyaistvo', *Voprosy Ekonomiki* (5)

Sidorenko, B. (1983) 'Nachalo perestroiki', *Ekonomicheskaya Gazeta* (25), 19

Simenenko, G. K. (1983) 'Na iskhodnoi pozitsii', *Ekonomicheskaya Gazeta* (51), 7

'Sistema material'no-tekhnicheskogo snabzheniya' (1969) *Ekonomicheskaya Gazeta* (40), 5

Skorodunov, E. (1966) 'O kachestve radiotovarov', *Sovetskaya Torgovlya* (9)

Smith, A. (1985) 'International trade and resources' in *The Domestic Roots of Soviet Foreign Policy*, Royal Institute of International Affairs, London

Sokolov, I. (1969) 'Podsobnye promysly: nuzhdy i perspektivy', *Sel'skaya Nov'* (11)

—— (1982) 'Lichnym khozyaistvam nuzhna pomoshch'', *Ekonomicheskaya Gazeta* (10), 19

Solomakha, A. (1983) 'Reservy severnoi nivy', *Ekonomischeskaya Gazeta* (24), 12

Solomin, V. (1977) 'Kachestvo planirovaniya i organizatsiya kapital'nogo stroitel'-stva', *Voprosy Ekonomiki* (1)

'S veterkom' (1968) *Pravda*, 2 December, p. 2

Szász, T. (1974) 'Osszefüggések a beruháshátékonyság és a beruházások koncentracios rendszere kozott', *Ipargazdasag, 26* (10), quoted in Hare (1979)

Tarasov, B. (1950) 'Otdel partiinogo komiteta ili khozyaistvennoe vedomstvo', *Pravda*, 29 July, p. 2

Tarnavskii, G. (1973) 'Obespechenie zakonnosti v dogovornykh otnosheniyakh kolkhozov', *Sotsialisticheskoe Zakonodatel'stvo* (7)

Telegin, V. (1983) 'Na brosovykh zemlyakh', *Ekonomicheskaya Gazeta* (24), 13

Tikhomirov, Yu. (1983) 'Edinstvo prav i obyazannoistei', *Ekonomicheskaya Gazeta* (38), 15

Tikhonov, N. A. (1984) 'Za protsvetanie sovetskoi rodiny', *Pravda*, 2 March, p. 2

Tipovaya Metodika Opredeleniya Ekonomicheskoi Effektivnosti Kapital'nykh Vlozhenii (1969), *Ekonomicheskaya Gazeta* (39)

Tipivaya Metodika Opredeleniya Ekonomicheskoi Effektivnosti Kapital'nykh Vlozhenii i Novoi Tekniki v Narodnom Khozyaistve SSSR (1960) *Gosplan SSSR, Akademiya Nauk SSR, Institut Ekonomiki*, Moscow

Trapeznikov, V. A. (1970) ' "Glagoli" upravleniya: znaet – mozhet – khochet – uspevaet', *Literaturnaya Gazeta*, 12 May

Trokhin, V. (1983) 'Agrarnye zaboty metallurgov', *Ekonomicheskaya Gazeta* (27), 18

Tsygankov, Yu. (1976) 'Effektivnost' nepreryvnogo planirovaniya kapital'nogo stroitel'stva', *Voprosy Ekonomiki* (2)

Tuganov, A. (1983) 'Trebovatel'nost' kollektiva', *Ekonomicheskaya Gazeta* (6), 9

Ulubaev, K. (1983) 'Pereshli na podryad', *Ekonomicheskaya Gazeta* (46), 17

'Uluchshat' planirovanie, organizatsiyu i upravlenie kapital'nym stroitel'stvom' (1984) *Ekonomika Stroitel'stva* (7)

'Uporyadochit' tekniko-ekonomicheskie obosnovaniya stroitel'stva' (1965) *Ekonomika Stroitel'stva* (11)

Urbanek, L. (1968) 'Some difficulties in implementing the economic reforms in Czechoslavakia', *Soviet Studies, 19* (4)

Utochkin, I. and Kuznetsov, M. (1970) 'Promysly – otasl' kolkhoznogo proizvodstva', *Ekonomika Sel'skogo Khozyaistva* (12)

Vaag, L. (1965) 'Effektivnost', interesovannost'', *Ekonomicheskaya Gazeta*, 20 October, pp. 8–9

Valovoi, D. and Nikitin, A. (1983) 'Posleslovie k zasedaniyu', *Pravda*, 23 November, p. 2

Varavka, V. (1975) 'Plan proizvodstva i portfel' zakazov', *Ekonomicheskaya Gazeta* (52), 14

Vasil'ev, F. (1968) 'S pozitsii khozyaistvennika', *Sel'skaya Nov'* (7), 10

Vasil'ev, G. (1983a) 'Zven'ya rabotayut na podryade', *Ekonomicheskaya Gazeta* (42), 16

—— (1983b) 'V otryve ot kompleksa', *Ekonomicheskaya Gazeta* (16), 16

Veselov, V. (1979) 'Podsobnoe lichnoe – ne lishnee', *Ekonomicheskaya Gazeta* (2), 19

'Višak nezaposlenih – i zaposlenih' (1982) *Ekonomska Politika*, 12 April, pp. 16-18

Vlaho, B. (1979a) 'Za dvije i pol godine – dva i pol puta veće', *Privredni Vjesnik*, 22 January, pp. 5-6

—— (1979b) 'Žilavi korijeni potrošnje', *Privredni Vjesnik*, 13 August, pp. 4-5

—— (1979c) 'Investiranje mimo plana', *Privredni Vjesnik*, 3 September, p. 9

Vlasov, V. G. (1984) 'Prava i otvetstvennost'', *Ekonomicheskaya Gazeta* (4), 7

Volkov, A. (1983) 'Po-novomu organizovali trud', *Ekonomicheskaya Gazeta* (31), 17

Vovchenko, N. (1965) 'Bystree osvaivat' proizvodstvennye moshchnosti', *Ekonomika Stroitel'stva* (10)

'V Tsentral'nom Komitete KPSS i Sovete Ministrov SSSR' (1982) *Ekonomicheskaya Gazeta* (23), special supplement

'V Tsentral'nom Komitete KPSS i Sovete Ministrov SSSR' (1983) *Ekonomicheskaya Gazeta* (31), 5

'V TsK KPSS i Sovete Ministrov SSSR' (1979) *Pravda*, 29 July, pp. 1-2

'V TsK KPSS, Sovete Ministrov i VTsSPS' (1983) *Ekonomicheskaya Gazeta* (33), 3-4

'Vypolnenie plana stroitel'stva – vazhneishaya narodno-khozyaistvennaya zadacha' (1972) in *Planovoe Khozyaistvo* (5)

Weitzman, M. (1980) 'The "ratchet principle" and performance incentives', *Bell Journal of Economics, 11* (1)

Wilber, C. K. (1969) *The Soviet Model and Underdeveloped Countries*, University of North Carolina Press, Chapel Hill, NC

Wiles, P. (1981) 'Wage and income policies' in L. Schapiro and J. Godson (eds.), *The Soviet Worker*, Macmillan, London

Yagodin, L. (1968) 'Tovarishch iz raikoma', *Ekonomicheskaya Gazeta* (44), 26

Yanowitch, M. (1977) *Social and Economic Inequality in the Soviet Union*, Martin Robertson, London

Yasinskii, G. (1973) 'Prokurorskii nadzor po delam o khishcheniyakh sotsialisticheskogo imushchestva', *Sotsialisticheskoe Zakondatel'stvo* (10)

Zakharov, Yu. and Petrov, N. (1974) 'Ob''edineniya segodnya', *Pravda*, 7 August, p. 2

Zakirov, Sh. N. (1965) *Voprosy Razvitiya i Razmeshcheniya Promyshlennosti Uzbekistana*, Nauka, USSR, Tashkent

Zangurashvili, V. (1976) 'V srok i polnost'yu', *Pravda*, 8 February, p. 3

'Zarabotnaya plata – po gotoroi produktsii' (1968) *Ekonomicheskaya Gazeta* (27), 20

Zaslavskaya, T. (1983) *Doklad o Neobkhodimosti Bolee Uglublennogo Izucheniya v SSSR Sostial'nogo Mekhanizma Razvitiya Ekonomiki*, Radio Liberty, *Materialy Samizdata* (35/83), 26 August, AC No. 5042

'Zašto nema udruživanja' (1981) *Ekonomska Politika*, 6 April, p. 12

INDEX